The Nurse in the Delivery Room Slapped Me... Once

Published in the United States by
Beckham Publications Group, Inc.
PO Box 4066, Silver Spring, MD 20914

Library of Congress Control Number: 2007921378

ISBN: 0-931761-25-5

The Nurse in the Delivery Room Slapped Me... Once

Stories and Perspectives
To Help You Unlock Your Amazing Potential

D Anthony

Silver Spring

Any uplifting insight derived from the life stories and assorted verses in this book—and, even more, any radical, be-true-to-yourself, find-your-purpose-and-go-for-it, spiritually-evolve, endeavor-to-be-happy-in-the-precious-time-we-have, believe-in-yourself-and-your-dreams, you-can-change-the-world inspired thoughts and deeds these passages might incite—are dedicated to the many people who have managed to touch me along the way, in particular a couple of loving souls who have been there for me since day one.

The folks who've touched me: Many of these individuals are known by name; however, countless more are not. Some of the stories and associated influences are reflected throughout this book, but many more are not. Yet from the best of friends, to the good natured stranger, to those willing to share their stories in the media, that others might grow, you've inspired me, proven that a positive attitude is addictive, strengthened my faith, and challenged me to be ever mindful of my destiny. And for that, I say, "Thank you."

The two individuals: A beautiful woman, loving and sacrificing in every way, from whom I would first learn the value of loved ones, tradition, humility, compassion, fellowship, simple pleasures, laughter, inner strength, and faith. And a man, strong and determined, from whom I would first learn the power of commitment, being willing to stand alone, standing for something, perseverance whatever the odds, consistency, work ethic, and pride. To these two people—from this point forward to be referred to simply as Mom and Dad—I say, "Thank you."

Every day is a blessing, and every blessing
a gift from God. Spend your blessings wisely.

–D Anthony

Contents

Introduction

This is a book of potential, faith, purpose, hopes and dreams. This is a book about the importance of time, the power of choice, growth, toughening up and having a heart, commitment, passion, and inspiration. This is a book that considers the ups and downs, life, and death—and what it all means. More than anything however, this is a book that considers a journey's impact, a life-long quest for meaning, happiness and fulfillment, and the resulting stories, perspectives, and lessons that I have collected along the way.

As it turns out, somehow in the midst of years of just trying to survive the excruciating heartache, disheartenment and sorrow that come with having someone you love with all your heart taken away, life began to take on a whole new meaning for me. I realized that life is fleeting. I realized that whether we utilize our time wisely, whether we believe in ourselves, whether we challenge our fears, whether we endeavor to reach for our dreams and aspirations, whether we strive to make a difference—one thing is certain: the sand will continue to fall through the hourglass, and one day will soon become the next.

So, in the time we have here, why wouldn't we choose to spend that time purposefully, striving for that which matters? Why wouldn't we want to live our lives dedicated to experiencing every bit of true happiness and fulfillment we could possibly acquire?

Perhaps you doubt that "true happiness and fulfillment" really exist, having long ago accepted these concepts as trumped-up illusions treasured only by people not living in the real world. A story comes to mind. Years ago, in passing, I asked a young boy how he was. He answered that he was doing "good" because he didn't have to go to school that day, continuing that he didn't like school and wished he were done. I asked him whether he realized the importance of school, adding that if he got good grades he could be anything he wanted to be. I asked if he could be anything, what he would choose. He responded, "You mean like a bus driver?"

Don't get me wrong, a bus driver is a perfectly honorable and respectable profession. I think the boy was working with a very limited perspective about his universe of options. His thought process wasn't along the lines of: *not interested in becoming a CEO, judge, doctor, astronaut, or a governor... I think I want to be a bus driver.* He simply wasn't aware he had so many other options. Sound familiar?

Perhaps your perspective is, after years of trying, that true happiness and fulfillment just isn't within you. Since I have a hard time believing that the Almighty indiscriminately gifted some of us with a magnificent, destiny-defining spark, and did not gift countless others, my suspicion is that we all have the potential within us. It's just a matter, for some, of unlocking the door so that the potential can be released.

I'd like to think that, so many years ago, having presented that young boy with a more opportunistic outlook and additional career options, that he went on to improve his life. I'd also like to think that the stories and perspectives in this book will help unlock your amazing new potential and very own unique and winning mindset.

Make no mistake about it, we are all interconnected and most everything has purpose. What I do today has impact on your tomorrow. And what you do tomorrow has impact on others and me the following day—for good or bad. My mother was called home *yesterday. Today* I wrote, and you're reading, this book. And if your heart and mind are open, if you possess a willingness to consider, embrace and incorporate—then happiness and fulfillment can be yours and we can all look forward to a brighter *tomorrow.*

About The Book

On many occasions, the question has been posed whether (paraphrasing) the intended purpose of my writing is inspiration to seek a more enlightened spiritual path; or, instead, a call for greater personal enlightenment, a license of sorts, to release the motivated, dynamic, and empowered individual within. Without any hesitation, my answer invariably is yes.

If the thoughts, anecdotes, and perspectives offered here become the catalyst for a decision that changes the world for the better, I'm pleased with that. If instead, it is your world, or even merely a couple of your days, that are enhanced, I'm pleased with that also. If the result is enhanced perspective that causes you to tell a loved one how much you care, or to reconnect with a long lost friend, I'm pleased with that. If, instead, the result is to speak more often to the people you encounter on the street, I'm pleased with that also. If the result is a life considerably more committed to spiritual growth and a better relationship with the Almighty, I'm pleased with that. If, instead, the result is a more solid commitment to your aspirations, a solemn promise that your fulfillment and intended destiny in life you will more purposefully seek, I'm pleased with that also.

Whatever the derived message, whatever the useful insight, whatever meaningful perspective there is to be acquired, any positive impact is just that—a positive impact—for you and the world. And if you've ever found yourself pondering what's going on, doubtful as to how things can possibly be turned around, whether with respect to the quality and direction of your life or with respect to the lack of brotherhood and consideration in the world at large, the solution may very well be relatively simple. When it's all said and done, perhaps what it's going to take to change things is a growing number of us—altering mindsets, altering attitudes, altering paradigms, altering perceptions, and thus, actual prospects—one individual, one day, one inspired interaction at a time.

And as we could all benefit from the use of a little enlightenment of spirit from time to time, you are encouraged to utilize this book as a readily accessible kick-start of inspiration when needed. You are encouraged to enlist this book as your very own life-affirming, life-enriching, self-empowering tool.

Before diving in, there are a few things worth noting to add a little context and further prepare you for what is to come.

- This book is comprised of thoughts, feelings, perspectives, and revelations about the purpose and relevance of life; a lifetime of happenstances and interactions, and the meaning ultimately derived.
- Just to be clear, I am not a doctor. I'm just someone who happens to be *blessed* with the need, from the time I was a child, to always ask why, and *cursed* with the need for a somewhat, at least, logical answer.
- The experiences, events, and assorted details related, intended to offer perspective and food for thought about the nature of life, are in no way presented in chronological order. As for the stories and passages, written over the course of numerous recent years; the first offered could have been the last written, and the last could have been the first. Intentionally, it is a testament to the randomness of life.
- Some thoughts, perspectives, and anecdotes shared will be reinforced many times throughout.

The repetitive nature is purposeful, as increased exposure will lead to increased absorption and adoption; ultimately fostering an even more fortified new you.

- Last, but not least, given this book is a collection of individual stories and verses, the original intent was for each to stand alone. It was envisioned that each item would be separately read and appropriately pondered for the incremental insight and perspective that each separately could potentially bring. But just the same, you can read it straight through from cover to cover, seek out particular chapters when in need, select randomly day to day, earmark favorites and read them whenever the mood strikes, or employ any combination of the above.

But however you employ this book, however you choose to use it, do use it. For, as far as we know, we've got one life to get it right. And the power to change is in our hands. And now, so is the book.

It's time to turn the page.

Impacted by a particular poem or story?
Share your thoughts at www.STSTheBook.com

The SomethingToShare Daily Affirmation

I affirm that on this day I will...

Take the time to listen to the rustling leaves,
And to the passing breeze that made them so,
Marvel at just a bit of the majestic beauty
In the world around me,
And in some way rediscover the innocence of my youth.

I will tell, or better yet show,
A loved one how much they mean to me,
Help someone in need,
Immerse myself in that, which inspires me,
Strengthen my faith in the Almighty,
And strive to be someone in whom
The Almighty can have faith in return.

I will smile each and every chance I get;
And, whenever I can, bring someone else along for the ride.
I will endeavor to be modest as a rule,
But audacious when called for.

I will always know that I am here for a purpose,
And I will respect and appreciate this day
For the blessed and amazing gift it is.
I affirm that the precious time I have this day
Will be spent wisely,
I affirm, this day, zestfully will be the way I live.

Born To Lead

We have zero probability of coming into our own or of achieving our intended destiny if we do not possess the desire, will, and fortitude to discover and chart our own course. To accomplish this we must define self, forge our own distinctive paths, become forces to be reckoned with, and believe in ourselves, no matter the odds. After all, in our own individual ways, we were all born to lead.

The Nurse in the Delivery Room Slapped Me... Once

See, here's the thing: I was minding my own business, so I did nothing to warrant what was forthcoming in any way. For the most part, things were pretty okay. Simply put, I was calmly and collectively working on figuring out where I was and what had happened to the dimly-lit, warm, serene, loving place I had, for so many months, come to call home. Then, all of a sudden, it happened...

You're not going to believe this, but for no apparent reason, this woman, whom I didn't know from Adam, lifts me up, smiles at me, then hauls off and slaps me. Okay, I'll admit it. I may have cried a little, at first. But hey, it surprised me and I had a lot going on at the time. Okay, I guess I'm digressing. Anyway, the point is the message was clear: Welcome to life!

Here's a newsflash. From time to time, most often when we're least expecting it, life is going to get in a good slap, punch, or kick. In some cases, it may be merely a stinger. In others, we just may find ourselves dazed, potentially even prone. So whatever the next ordeal, whether the death of a loved one, illness, natural disaster, random mishap, love unrequited, day-to-day strife, or plain old general despair, it's not a matter of *if* it will occur, but *when.* No matter how guarded, how diligent, how positive, or how motivated we endeavor to be, from time to time, life is going to find a way of happening to each of us—again. However, that's not to say there is a need for despair. For, much the same way I would suspect, as any experienced trainer prepares an unseasoned boxer, the message is simple: No matter how good you are, sooner or later a good punch will inevitably find you. And when that happens, the canvas may, at least for a few moments, be your only friend. But when it happens, if you find yourself no longer in an upright position, if your senses should momentarily take a back seat to the cobwebs that have taken up temporary residence in your mind, don't just lie there stunned in disbelief, feeling sorry for yourself, regretfully contemplating what could or should have been done. Get up! Get up and, on an equal plain, introduce your adversary to the face of renewed determination and unfettered will. Let your heart, fortitude, and intensified determination leave no trace of doubt—you've taken your opponent's best shot and you are back, more motivated and committed than ever. The immensity of the moment will begin to set in as you sense the tables starting to turn. The energy will surge inside of you, as across your face appears to be just a hint of a grin. And why not? It is, after all, time you dished out a little punishment of your own.

The bottom line is our destiny in this life is ultimately up to us. It's our choice. Each of us can be a perennial victor, perpetual victim, or something in between. Each of us can be a worthy combatant with a winning attitude or something considerably less with a whining attitude. The reality is the daily choices we make, and therefore our ultimate potential in life is completely up to each and every one of us.

Which leads to the question: The next time life happens to you, the next time you feel the sting of a convincing punch, the next time your posterior has firsthand knowledge of the canvas, how will you respond? Will you just lie there dazed and confused, intent on collecting excuses, wondering why the past was; maybe preoccupied with the notion that bad luck happens only to you? Or, instead, will you accept nothing less than ownership of your circumstances, choose to stand and demand more from yourself and your life? Are you prepared, or better yet, are you committed enough to take charge of your present and your future?

What choice will you make?

I can only tell you that my choice was made early on. The nurse in the delivery room slapped me, but only once...

> Real success can be measured only by way of opportunities made, not opportunities granted.

A World of Change

Changing the world—that's a pretty audacious concept. How can such a grand idea be possible? How is it possible that impact meaningful to a whole world could possibly emanate from an individual? After all, the world is a rather massive place. And a pretty convincing argument can be made that, comparatively speaking, we are pretty small. However, one shouldn't make the mistake of equating relative size with relative significance, much less relative potential to change the world. Instead, insofar as making a difference is concerned, it effectively comes down to the degree of commitment, dedication to purpose, and persistence demonstrated in the face of whatever odds, across whatever the span of time required. Merely a few tiny termites, unchecked, over time, are more than adequate testament to this reality, regardless of the magnitude or perceived significance of the structure inevitably at risk.

Not only can one individual make a difference well beyond what would generally be thought of as his, or her, perceivable reach, in effect, impact and otherwise change the world as we know it, but individuals do change the world, and on a much more frequent basis than most of us have ever begun to imagine. Think about it, as a rule of thumb, it's pretty unlikely for many people to come up with the same idea at the same time. Our minds simply aren't connected that way. As a result, it's a pretty good bet that every discovery, every invention, every physical and conceptual advancement, every concept or construct that has ever made a difference in our lives and the lives of countless others had to originate with an appropriately inspired individual, primed with a soon to be evolutionary thought.

Just take a couple of seconds and look around you. Chances are virtually everything you can see, hear, touch or feel is a reflection of this phenomenon—and, in the majority of cases, not just once. Subsequent to initial conception, many of the items around you have been enhanced or elevated on numerous occasions, in numerous ways. Each and every improvement, every meaningful enhancement to every existing object, idea, or belief; every forthcoming initiative with the promise of widespread improvement to come was born from an individual thought, first conceived by an individual achiever.

Virtually everything you've ever learned, come to perceive and believe, and, to some extent, come to be is a reflection of this phenomenon. The very fact that you can read this passage and the fact that I could write it evidences that we are each living testaments to the power and the ultimate potential of this phenomenon. From Mother Teresa to Madonna, from William Shakespeare to Bill Gates, from Julius Erving to Julius Caesar, from Albert Einstein to Nelson Mandela, from Bill Clinton to the guy who created Post-it Notes, each of these individuals has, through idea, belief, and deed, affected countless people, single-handedly, in their own unique way, changing the world we know.

With all the evidence around us, once and for all, let us eliminate all doubt. You can, I can, we *can* change the world!

One of my favorite stories, illustrating the extent of impact an individual can have on the world simply by believing in himself, and not giving up on his dream, is one of a late blooming businessman.

As the story goes, recently retired, the gentleman realized he was going to have great difficulty surviving on the limited monthly income he was receiving. As a result, he feverishly searched for something else he could possibly do, or something else he possessed, that might yield value and sufficiently enhance his financial outlook for the remainder of his life. Ultimately, he determined the one item of potential value he had was a recipe for fried chicken, extremely popular with family and friends.

He set out to make a deal with any restaurant that would entertain his business proposition. He offered to give each restaurant his recipe for free, for a percentage of incremental revenue generated by chicken sales. He received one successive rejection after the next, eventually packing up much of his belongings for an extended road trip. Legend has it that his rejection count was just shy of one thousand by the time a restaurant decided to give his offer a chance. The rest, as they say, is history—as the recipe, the gentleman, and the resulting business went on to be a tremendous, worldwide success.

And despite the fact that the gentleman is no longer living, even today, he continues to impact countless people around the world everyday—customers, employees, stockholders, distributors, and many of their families. People eat, families get a little closer, entrepreneurs own businesses, employees earn salaries, bills are paid, refrigerators are stocked, teenagers find part-time employment, all because of a very determined gentleman armed with motivation, a dream, and a chicken recipe. As a matter of fact, if you are at least an occasional consumer of fast food chicken, odds are pretty good that you too can be counted among the many that have been impacted, that you as well have, at some point, had the pleasure of sampling Kentucky's finest.

Because one man, likely more senior in years than you, in desperate financial straits effectively transformed his one potentially bankable asset into a viable dream, then fostered and maintained the degree of passion necessary to see it through, the world can never be the same. And if he could do it—commit to himself, find his purpose, live for his dream, and not accept failure as an option—what exactly is stopping you and me?

So what is your intended purpose? What is the bankable asset you have that can motivate you and positively affect the lives in the world around you? What will it take for your dream to become meaningful to others? Do you have what it takes to be committed and see it through? Whatever it is, modest or audacious, long or short-term, concentrated or widespread, now is the time to begin. The sooner you, and the individuals around you, can begin to be changed, the sooner others can be changed in turn. The sooner you get started, the sooner your intended destiny can begin to be fulfilled. The sooner you get started, the sooner your impact on the world, in earnest, can take root and begin to grow.

In the immortal words of the lyrical philosopher Teddy Pendergras: "The world won't get no better, if we just let it be, the world won't get no better, we've got to change it—just you and me."

> Attitude is like seasoning. Under-use is bland. Overuse is unpalatable. However, in just the right proportion...

Who I Am

Listening to a commercial one day, I noticed an irony that, no doubt, escaped much, if not all of, the remainder of the listening audience. The advertisement offered the perspective that a watch is about the most individual item that a person can possess, that it, beyond anything else, provides the most significant insight into the personal style and personality of its owner. The commercial closed with the store's invitation for listeners to visit so a specialist could present the perfect watch for them.

I thought, *Okay, what am I missing*? If the watch is such an important indicator of the type of individual I am, why exactly would I ever need, or desire for that matter, someone else to select the best anything for me, especially someone who doesn't even know me? How could anyone be better equipped for determining what *is* me *than* me? And given the advantage of the ultimate inside track knowing me far beyond the level that anyone else even begins to, why would I ever choose to abdicate that role to anyone else?

Unfortunately, my guess is that a significant percentage of the listeners would have been fine with someone else making this type of decision. Why is that my perception? Well, just think about the extent to which this is demonstrated by many of the choices made on a daily basis, from excitement over the latest "in" clothing, as dictated by the latest "in" popular designer, to being unduly influenced by the latest superstar's funded endorsement; from the influence of omnipresent commercial advertisements to the effects of questionable political ads with unfortunately massive public opinion-swaying power; from, virtually blind acceptance of anything heard, seen, or read in the media to the far too meaningful cliques in our personal and professional lives. The bottom line is that we seem to have a burning need to be told what to think and do.

We often willingly accept the barrage of people and organizations, all on a daily basis, actively endeavoring to define for us what's best, how we feel, and who we are—or at least who we should want to be. Worse, beyond merely accepting it, we have grown to depend on it.

Watching a town hall meeting some time back, a question was posed (I'm paraphrasing): Which was of greater concern in their lives—the problems with the U.S. economy or a particular dictator clear across the other side of the world? Nearly everyone chose the U.S. government foe. Only a few of the sixty or so people indicated the economy. Now, I'm all for the collective value of differing opinions, but it strikes me as peculiar that, given the significantly depressed stock market the previous year, lost family nest-eggs, significantly reduced consumer spending, and a slumping job market, how a regime clear across the world, which had been relatively quiet and pretty boxed in politically and militarily for the better part of a decade, and which most likely had had discernable impact on few of the audience members' lives, if any, could be of greater concern.

What was the possibility that town-hall participants had been influenced by the administration's recent blanketing of airwaves with unsubstantiated omens about an immanent threat to the free world? And what was the possibility that the media's ratings-based, sensationalized coverage, perpetuated daily with the help of incendiary phrases like "Countdown to War," further influenced those in attendance? That couldn't have been what caused all the folks in the town hall to raise their hands, could it? Interestingly enough, I even noticed one audience member who seemingly wasn't going to raise her hand, but did when she witnessed virtually everyone else with their hands in the air.

How did we get to this point? Well, it seems somewhere along the way we began to abdicate responsibility for the decisions in our life, and slowly but surely it became more and more acceptable that we take that easier route. It seems that, as a society, we are losing a little more ground each day.

As parents, we abdicate to the school systems too often, to some best selling child psychologist (in many cases well-versed in parental case studies, yet unable to reach the children in their household), or, worse, the child him or herself. As citizens, we are too often willing to abdicate our stance on the relevant issues of the day to the perspectives of virtually anyone with notoriety, and sometimes merely anyone with a microphone, from politicians to radio disc jockeys, from religious leaders to the press (seemingly effortlessly able to ride the dependable waves of innuendo and sensationalism when facts alone can't supply the requisite ripple in public opinion). As individuals, we too often abdicate to friends and acquaintances, regularly subjugating our views to the whims of the group. And we too often abdicate to our employers whom we sometimes allow to define us and too significantly influence who we aspire to be.

Simply put, on a daily basis, many of us too readily abdicate responsibility for the defining decisions in our lives. Big or small, too often we are alarmingly content with allowing avoidance to be our only course of action, happenstance the outcome. Unfortunately, however, while it's true you don't have to worry about the possibility of striking out if you never step up to bat, you'll also never know the glory of getting a base hit, not to mention hitting a homerun. And, ultimately, our lives are supposed to be about playing the game, not riding the bleachers, watching everyone else play the game for us.

Increasingly, the difficulty is the fact that society not only condones lack of personal thought and expression but often encourages it. Think about it. Would most of your family, friends, neighbors, coworkers, managers, and acquaintances prefer the assertive, self-defined you, or the you that fits the proverbial "don't worry, be happy" mold? Given the choice, my theory is most people would opt for the easier-to-convince, less-engaged you. That you, after all, is much easier to influence and manipulate.

Conditioning often begins at an early age and continues throughout life. For example, have you ever asked a young child, who is just learning to express himself, a question and heard the parent say, "Tell Mr. So-And-So, that's because...?" (Personally, it's one of the little things that make my skin crawl.)

In the school system, children are primarily rewarded based on their ability to regurgitate text from the manual and verse from the instructor, not their capability to think and question. Try asking the child questions about why the topic matters and what it means. (In some cases, try asking the instructor for that matter.)

I heard an explanation once about how the circus is able to so easily restrain an adult elephant. Typically, merely one of the animal's massive legs can be bound to a small tree with the lightest of ropes. Why doesn't the massive, incredibly strong animal simply break away from the weak constraint? As it turns out, the answer is pretty simple: When the elephant was much younger, and, obviously, much weaker, the handlers would utilize a heavy chain to bind its leg to a sizeable tree trunk. No matter how much the young elephant struggled, it learned it could not get away. Eventually, this created a life-limiting perception that whenever its leg is bound, no escape is possible. So the actual confinement in the conditioned adult elephant is not so much physical as it is psychological.

As a result, we should be extremely careful about the subliminal lessons we subscribe to ourselves, not to mention those taught to our children. There is a Gladys Knight song, which begins with the lyric, "To fulfill the need to be who I am in this world is all I ask." There's a message for our youth: Find out who you are. Stand for something. Have an opinion.

Our true destinies in life can not begin to be fulfilled until we at least begin to define ourselves. And the first step is to learn to be true to ourselves, regardless of the circumstance.

When it's all said and done, no one else can define you. That is an obligation and privilege that only you can truly fulfill, but only if you choose to. So get out there and find your own watch.

> Nothing infests, and ultimately eradicates, any and every trace of a dream or aspiration with quite the toxicity of complacency. Handle with extreme caution anytime you find it in your midst.

When Things Are Unfair

Take a few moments and make a quick mental list of some of the truly successful people you've known... Now, narrow that list down to the most successful person you've ever encountered—in particular, the individual you most perceive to be more personally fulfilled than yourself. Would you describe that person as engaged... energized... challenged... and passionate about his or her efforts and defining purpose? Would you describe that person as inspired... enthusiastic... encouraging... and full of life, and promise, for the future? If a truly successful, fulfilled individual was identified, it's likely the answer is a resounding yes to all the above.

For these individuals, attitude breeds true success, not the superficial variety typically defined by financial standing or title, but the intrinsic kind that both defines and lifts the soul, then touches the hearts and souls of others. For these individuals, a degree of success is achieved that ultimately breeds a lasting sense of fulfillment in every facet of their life.

It's fair to say, however, that there are many who don't exhibit, or even seem to in any way possess, the aforementioned traits or the motivated outlook on behalf of the future. As a result of this void in perspective, members of this contingent unknowingly often forfeit opportunities otherwise there for the taking.

Exactly why is that?

Is it possible the individuals, fortunate enough to possess these traits and associated mindsets, simply are the Almighty's favorites, unfairly singled out to be the recipients of eternal blessings that bolster their every attempted task? Have these individuals been secretly slipped the Cliff's Notes for the *Definitive*

Guide to a Successful Life while the rest of us either get no reference, or are forced to wade through the painstakingly difficult volumes? For these individuals, as a rule, does little effort produce tremendous reward, is disappointment not a familiar acquaintance, does it tend to rain only on days their umbrella is remembered?

While these cynic-laced perspectives don't even begin to correlate with reality, it does seem that these people often are able to reap twice the reward for half the effort. And if this is the case, then doesn't that at least indicate that there is some degree of unfairness, or at least an unnatural imbalance in outcome and benefits awarded?

Absolutely not.

More often than not, when we fail to achieve any discernable progress from our efforts, when perspective readily becomes acceptance that failure will be yet another endeavor's likely end, it has little to do with fate, chance, or equivalency to the Almighty's second-class step-children.

No, in reality there is one place to look when we are continuously striking out—or worse, when we get to the point that we refuse to even get up to bat. You see, if we continuously remain hitless, half-heartedly swinging, or maybe closing our eyes as the ball arrives, if we never adapt or learn from our experiences, never attempting the necessary adjustments, with an ever more prevalent mindset that someone else, or something else, is to blame, failure, and ultimately disillusionment will be our self-fulfilled reward.

Should there be a need for assignment of blame for lack of perseverance and continued futility, there is no need to look any farther than the nearest mirror. It's not the fault of the opposing team, the bat, the ball, the wind, the jeering crowd, or any other extraneous, yet convenient, excuse. In the end, the responsibility and the potential for change belongs to each and every one of us.

Success, more than anything, comes from having a winning mindset. And the difference between people with a winning mindset and people without is that people without a winning mindset believe the race to be imbalanced before the gun is fired. The people with a winning mindset know that imbalance has everything to do with their attitude, effort, and perseverance both before and after the first hint of the starter pistol is heard.

The fact is, by rule there is imbalance in life. It is said, for example, that by the laws of nature, no two things can be equal. Successful people, more often than not, find a way of having the imbalance tilt in their favor. Ultimately, any advantage is not so much an advantage granted or awarded as an advantage achieved, or earned.

In the end there is a non-coincidental, perfectly logical, and certainly other than divine reason why successful people, in effect, can acquire twice the reward with seemingly half the effort. They possess the presence of mind, attitude, and perseverance to more efficiently and effectively accomplish their objectives, maintaining a positive outlook, never permitting doubt to sufficiently take root, learning from their mistakes, keeping it all in perspective and enjoying the ride along the way. This mindset and approach to life consistently affords them tremendous advantages in addressing and often avoiding otherwise derailing roadblocks. As a result, it is this incredibly empowering perspective that supplies these individuals with their truly enviable ability to transcend their dreams and aspirations into reality. You may still wonder how such an advantage can be fair.

Simply put, fair does not require that everyone possess the same mindset and capabilities. That would suggest that we would all need to be equal, a scenario not so feasible given nature's laws. Fairness, instead, is reflected in the fact that we have all been blessed with the ability to nurture and expand these attributes and mindsets. And fortunately, it's never too late to start.

When things just don't seem fair, it's important to remember that equal was never intended to be. As opposed to sulking or complaining, realize the power to enhance your standing resides within you, buying into the notion that the better your mindset, the better your choices, and the better your choices, the better the results—continually endeavor to hone and elevate your attitude and perspective. In time, you will find yourself being transformed, ever closer to your true potential, ever closer to an example others site among the most successful individuals they know.

Are there simply different types of successful people? Most definitely, there are those who have tapped into the empowering, innate, fundamental desire common to all the Almighty's creations to fulfill their purposes in life and those who, as of yet, have not.

And as a rule of thumb, individuals who have tapped into this innate need are too focused on enhancing their daily perspective, challenging past limitations, passionately pursuing dreams and aspirations, and succumbing to an ever growing and unquenchable desire to evolve, to get at least a taste of their true destiny, to waste any time pondering about why life isn't fair. If you are spending any time worrying about the extent to which things seem unfair, well...

Take a few moments and make a quick mental list of some of the truly successful people you've known. Are you on that list? If not, are you prepared to take the necessary steps to begin to get there? If not, then any unfairness in life would seem to have little to do with divine choice—and everything to do with your choice.

In other words, if, in the future, you should ever discover why things haven't been fair don't be surprised if the real culprit is someone you are intimately familiar with, someone you aren't likely to find on your list.

> Quality is a mark of distinctive excellence attainable only through dedication, effort, and concern.

How're You Looking?

I had endeavored not to hold back anything, not to leave any stone unturned in my committed attempt to encourage and inspire a fellow coworker who was deeply concerned about the viability of his job given the recent company announcement of a merger and imminent downsizing of the combined workforce. I told him that he was uniquely qualified, as he was highly skilled in a discipline that would most certainly continue to be just as important to the integrated company. Further, I suggested that because he was fortunate enough to have been able to develop such a distinctive skill set and working expertise in a business-critical area, his qualifications would likely make him very marketable to numerous other companies. In fact, I suggested that perhaps this might offer him a great opportunity to test the recruitment waters, to ideally seize this as a blessing in disguise, a unique opportunity to reshape and redefine his career as well as the extent of his potential. The conversation would go just a little further before it drew to an end. As we were finishing up, I commented that he didn't look happy. He responded, "What is there to be happy about?"

Have you ever noticed how self-fulfilling the prophecy of life tends to be? It seems that what we expect out of each situation, each minute, each day, out of life, is– what we typically get. When we consistently focus on the best, expect the best, strive for the best, are our best, and combine that expectation with appropriate effort, the odds are good that the best outcomes will befall us. Conversely, if we focus, expect, or strive for anything less, regardless of the extent of our associated effort, the odds are almost certain that the resulting opportunities and outcomes will duly reflect those limited expectations.

Similarly, when life's only perceived objective is to unload on you, when seemingly one bad stretch after another is the only kind of luck you can manage to find, that is most definitely not the time to hang your head. If anything, getting frustrated and hanging your head will only make the issue worse. The simple truth is, people truly destined for success don't tend to spend a lot of time feeling sorry for themselves. Instead of being viewed as a collection of overbearing hardships, as a continuous ominous downpour forever overshadowing every hint of opportunity and potential progress, for people destined to have success, these challenges are perceived in a considerably more beneficial manner.

Careful not to perceive them as more daunting than they truly are, each challenge is individually dissected in an effort to comprehend its origin and root cause. Not only is this vital for resolving the current issue but also for minimizing the opportunity for a repeat occurrence. At this point, the people destined for the most success do something incredibly unique. Before the problem is resolved, while the extent of the pain, the heartache, the feelings of loss, the embarrassment, the loneliness, the self-doubt, the guilt, the sorrow, the frustration, the disdain are raw and fresh in their minds, hearts and consciousnesses, they ask themselves vital questions: *What purpose is there for me, being in this situation, here and now? What lesson am I intended to learn? What meaningful knowledge and insight does this challenge offer to strengthen and ultimately propel me?*

Not only does this approach foster the perspective that issues are disconnected and individual, and so considerably easier to solve, it serves to eliminate reoccurrence and effectively enhances not only one's outlook but also one's potential for the future. In the end, while many are hampered and/or stagnated by each new difficult and seemingly insurmountable issue, these fortunate individuals instinctively use these life experiences as they are intended—as the means and the motivation to grow.

The bottom line is, sometimes when you're least expecting, life is going to knock you down. The question is: How will you respond? At those times, will you tend to dwell on the misfortune, the drought of fairness that has deposited the latest issue at your doorstep? Or will you endeavor to capitalize on your circumstances, potentially even growing a little in the process? As Les Brown, one of the most inspiring and entertaining motivational speakers I've seen, so passionately and succinctly puts it: "When life knocks you down, remember you have to look up to get up."

Absolutely nothing in this life has ever knocked me down with the force and intensity, with the degree of utter heartache and sorrow, as the loss of my mother. The person I loved most, the one who seemingly never focused on her own happiness primarily because she was always concerned about everyone else, was unjustly and unceremoniously taken. There was no apparent rhyme or reason. It simply wasn't fair. There was bitterness. There was disdain. But most of all there was pain. My feelings of loss were so deep and severe; I quickly came to know why heartache had that name. My heartache, at times, seemed so overwhelming that, on at least a couple of occasions, I seriously questioned whether I truly wanted to live.

In the span of her passing, I went from loving practically everything about life to having no optimism or hope for the future. After all, what was the point? As much as I thought I was shaking it, as much as I tried to simply get back to the way things had been, I was just going through the motions. I went to work. I came home. The bills got paid. Family and friends couldn't quite reach me.

It wasn't until I began to consider what the real purpose of it all was, what meaning I was intended to derive, that things began to crystallize for me. It was true my mother was gone, and she wasn't coming back. It was true I still, well over a year later, missed her immensely and wished that she were still here. It was true that I wished she had had more time, had just been able to simply enjoy life at least a little more. I realized, however, it was also true that she wouldn't want me to continue feeling sorry about the situation, essentially wasting my life. No, she would want me to harness my faith, will, drive, and conviction to overcome my grief and find a way to be a better person. I discovered that not only was writing extremely cathartic for me, it had the potential to be liberating, motivational, and cathartic for others. From the depths of my greatest sorrow, the greatest meaning and the greatest purpose was there to be found, but only once I began to look up. I've been writing ever since.

The simple and inevitable truth is, from time to time, life is going to knock us down. Every once in a while, it's going to pack a punch the likes of which we've never seen or, more appropriately, we've never felt. Perhaps the purpose is to keep us at least somewhat humble, to teach us needed lessons or to encourage us to find a better way. Perhaps the purpose is merely to remind us never to cease appreciating the blessings we're fortunate enough to have. Whatever the intended purpose for the hardships that find their way into our lives, our ability to minimize the potential adverse psychological and emotional impacts, while concurrently ensuring growth and optimum positive influence from the lessons learned along the way, is primarily attributable to one factor: the nature of our response. What meaning is there to be found? What purpose is there that can cause us to begin to look up? How can we again begin to stand and, in the process, ultimately be even better than we were before we were ever knocked down?

Just know that, in the end, it's up to each and every one of us. Every day, in virtually every way, it is our choice. Each morning as we awake, just as consciousness begins to assume hold of our senses and we become cognitive of the new day, whether we realize it or not, each of us are again subconsciously presented with a question of incredible consequence, a consideration that will most assuredly influence our path, not only as we say goodbye to our respective pillows but even more importantly, for the remainder of the day. The question: Will this be a good day?

And here's the great news: It doesn't have to matter how we may have answered the question the last time or on any other preceding occasion. It doesn't have to matter what issues, missteps, or mistakes may have taken place. It doesn't have to matter what went unchecked on the to-do list yesterday, or how challenging the agenda for today is perceived to be. It only really matters how we choose to answer the question on this day.

Make no mistake about it, the direction we move in life is dictated most by the path we set for ourselves, whether we choose to look back or forward, whether we choose to look down or up. It makes perfect sense. Think about it. What typically happens when we choose to walk somewhere? First we decide where we want to go. Then we look in the direction we are going. Why should where we are destined to go in life be any different?

When it's all said and done, a lot of people spend a lot of their lives concerned about where they are, and worrying about where they've been. Perhaps more relevantly we should begin to focus on something considerably less daunting and immensely more important, like where we're going.

So tell me, how're you looking?

> Everyone is an artist. Finding your canvas is the key.

An Inspirational Lady

At about the age of nine, I happened upon a book in the school library, a little rhyming book with a simple message. To this day, as I think back on it, I'm amazed that the book had any discernable impression on me at all.

I was a young, inner-city kid with little to nothing in common with the senior heroine, living in what appeared to be an English kingdom during the Middle Ages. While she didn't have many friends, she did have one thing that was extremely important to her: a love for roller-skating. She would skate day in and day out. Skating was not only something she loved to do, but more, it was who she was.

Her neighbors didn't understand. Beyond failing to comprehend why a grown woman would commit her time to roller-skating instead of a respectable activity befitting a woman of her advanced age, they believed her behavior was rather silly. They ridiculed and laughed at her. But it didn't faze her. All that mattered to her was doing what she enjoyed, and she wasn't in need of anyone else's blessing.

Eventually, an opportunity arose in the kingdom. The king was in search of a woman who could solve his problem. The staff caring for the castle and royal family had grown so massive that there was no longer enough food, space, and peace and quiet for the royal family. Given all the clutter and chaos existing in the castle, the king was convinced there simply had to be a better way. As a result, a contest was proclaimed. Anyone who could prove themselves worthy and solve the king's problem would become rich in the process.

Because of the size of the award, every woman in town showed up, each trying to prove she was the rightful recipient of the riches. It wasn't long before things were out of control with considerably more noise and clutter throughout the castle. Finally, the king lost it. He yelled out, "Halt!" demanding the situation was much worse than anything they had seen. The women stood motionless, stopped dead in their tracks, all except one. You guessed it. The one individual in motion was that non-conformist Miss Tessie Tate. Miss Tessie Tate had been quietly, and most efficiently, going about her business, gliding on her skates. She was wiping down the walls, mopping the floors. In minimal time she declared the first floor to be complete. She was not only making short work of it but appeared to be having a good deal of fun in the process. Well, that was enough for the king to declare the winner of the riches.

Once Miss Tessie Tate won the contest, things in the town changed somewhat. The women developed a new level of respect for both Miss Tessie Tate and her little hobby. As the story comes to an end, we find Miss Tessie Tate is doing just fine. She is still doing what she loves, but a couple days a week she is doing it while cleaning the castle. The royal family is happy. Most interesting, however, are the town's women who, it seems, have taken up a new hobby.

It was just a simple little rhyming book, with a simple little message that I happened across in the library in fourth grade. It was a little rhyming book, with a simple message, that I must have checked out about three or four times and learned by heart.

I went on to finish elementary school, middle school, high school, and college. After embarking on a career, a conversation caused me to remember Miss Tessie Tate. Recalling the extent of interest exhibited, I began a search for a personal edition of the book. The book was no longer in print and inquiries to my elementary school library for information went unsatisfied. The librarian had not even heard of *Miss Tessie Tate.* (How can she consider herself a true elementary school librarian, interested in the development of young minds, and not be aware of a great masterpiece like *Miss Tessie Tate*? But I digress.)

Eventually, a book search service was able to track a copy down for me. When I received the message, the warning was: "We found it, but it's going to be costly." Little did the seller know that I would have paid much more than the thirty-five-dollar asking price for what I had come to remember as an important, if not yet completely understood, building block from my childhood. Well, the book arrived a few days later and, once again, I sat and enjoyed the little rhyming book with the simple message.

Ironically, it was not until that point, so many years later, that I really began to understand and appreciate what her story had meant to me decades ago. In the end, *Miss Tessie Tate* wasn't so much about a senior English woman or roller-skating as it was about just being true to who you are. It was about coming to understand and be happy with who you are. It was about the power of self-determination. It was about deciding the direction that was best for you and not letting anyone turn you around.

These were the inspiring, complex ideas behind the simple message in the little rhyming book, *Miss Tessie Tate.* It was this message that I now understand attracted me to that peculiar little book as a nine-year-old. And it was this inspiring, complex idea that I believe has been a part of me, as a source of personal strength, for each of the years since. And for that, I salute and thank the author, Jean Horton Berg.

I now understand that book's empowering concept provided an additional source of validation and personal power for every contentious situation since my adolescence. It is an empowering perspective that, over the years, has helped me more effectively and completely define myself.

Considering all of this, I found myself wondering whether this simple little rhyming book, with its newly comprehended complex and inspiring ideas, had made a similar impact on others. I wondered if any other adults were able to trace important elements of their core beliefs to this or any other children's book. I wondered if I would have been materially different had I not received this message as a nine-year-old from *Miss Tessie Tate.*

Further, I wondered how much different our youth would be if school systems mandated inspirational and motivational reading materials as part of the required curriculum. How much would this generation, and future ones, benefit from a steady stream of input that encourages self-confidence, self-reliance, perseverance, the importance of creativity, commitment to beliefs, the need to stand for something, the power to change self, and the power to change the world. It seems to me that these messages would represent an incredibly uplifting springboard, empowering young people to considerably greater heights and deeds.

I'm reminded of a fascinating psychology case study. Two groups of dogs were introduced to an experiment room with a bell, electrically chargeable floor, a lever, and a trap door leading to another room. The first group was individually led to the room with the lever and trap door de-activated; the second group had an activated door.

For the first group, once the bell sounded and the floor was charged, the lever was not activated. Each dog jumped around hitting up against the walls and lever for some period of time. Eventually, each dog would simply lie down and whimper. Subsequent trips would incur less jumping and earlier bouts of whimpering. In time, each of these dogs began to just lie down and whimper as soon as they heard the bell sound. After this point, subsequent efforts to train the dogs to use the lever to activate the trap door, even to utilize an open trap door, were only minimally successful, and only after significant quantities of attempts.

Dogs from the second group were individually introduced to the room with the lever activated. The bell would sound, the lever would activate, and the floor would charge, causing each of them to jump around in a similar manner. Upon hitting up against the lever, however, the trap door would open and the dog would escape to the connected room. Each of these dogs with successive trips quickly graduated to the point that, upon being led into the room, they would position themselves next to the lever. As soon as the bell sounded they would pull down the lever and exit to the adjoined room.

I found this to be an amazing case study with considerable implications for the human spirit. While the difference in the room was simply the activation of the lever, the ultimate difference in the subjects was the determination of whether they were the masters of their own destinies. Although not addressed in the case study, my guess is those dogs went on to be much more confident, happy, and successful in other activities attempted. My guess is a subset of the second group went on to become the leaders of the pack.

Success and fulfillment come down to having options. The more you believe you can generate and directly influence your own opportunities, the more you believe you have the power to control your own outlook on and circumstances in life, the more empowered you are to create your own self-fulfilling reality for an inspired and happy life.

On various occasions, I have pondered what distinguished me from so many of my friends and classmates who, upon transitioning into adulthood, never traveled in the direction of their aspirations and dreams. Perhaps the difference was that I never learned my lever wasn't activated. I know I owe a portion of that to the people and influences around me throughout the course of my life. And I believe I owe a portion of that to one particular inspirational lady in my life, Miss Tessie Tate.

Recently, I found myself in a heartfelt discussion with a good friend. After considerable dialogue, she challenged me, "What do you mean you don't need anyone's validation for anything that you do?" She went on, "That's not true. You need validation, everyone needs validation!" I confirmed she had a few more minutes to spare and I began to read: "There was an old lady named Miss Tessie Tate / Who'd been roller-skating e'er since she was eight..."

With the right attitude, this day anything is possible.

No Time Like Commitment

How committed are you to your hopes and dreams? How committed are you to your aspirations? How committed are you to your happiness and fulfillment? How committed are you to yourself?

How much free time did you have yesterday? In other words, how many unspoken-for minutes and hours did you accumulate throughout the day and evening with nothing vital or mandatory scheduled, off your employer's clock, with no meaningful obligations or prior commitments to fulfill?

Take a couple seconds and think back to yesterday. How much free time did you really have? It's likely that at least some of this time can be traced back to too-familiar pastimes that entice us, resulting in significant chunks of otherwise potentially productive time sacrificed in their wake. Culprits include the telephone, television, video games, recreational reading, and general recreation, to name a few.

While, in moderation, these activities can offer a healthy, occasional diversion from the hectic pace and demands of an otherwise unduly stressed life, it's too regular and extended investments of time that should make yesterday's "time that could have been better spent" tally.

Likewise, a quick audit of everyday events, tasks, and activities such as the work lunch hour, travel time, sleep schedule, and general down time (between other activities) will most likely yield additional instances of "time that could have been better spent." Just imagine the inroads you could have achieved yesterday, for instance, if you had simply committed your commute time and/or your lunch hour to consider, think about, plan, or strategize your available options and next steps.

Even more, just imagine what the impact could have been if you had simply, purposely, decided to reduce your sleep time by fifteen or twenty minutes, committing the time instead to brainstorming things you could accomplish the next day, propelling you ever closer to true happiness and fulfillment.

In the end, there's little doubt. Consistently committing at least a little of the time, which would otherwise be wasted, to your aspirations can make a world of difference. And if your dreams and aspirations are important to you, if the potential for true happiness and fulfillment is reason enough to care, now is the time to commit time and yourself to your future, to your destiny. No more excuses, misallocated blame, psychological crutches, or plain old avoidance, and no more justifications for delay. Now is the time.

- ### With Just a Little Time

With each meaningful task and objective achieved, with each once-mere possibility that becomes a sure thing, with the development of each new promise, idea, and opportunity that is integrated into your plan, an immensely valuable supply of inspiration is generated. This inspiration will, on a continuous basis, fuel your motivation, replenishing your store of commitment, continuously conditioning that commitment to strengthen and grow.

It is vital to commit at least a portion of your free time to these activities this day and every day that follows. Do this, and each day you will find yourself more and more fulfilled, and further along the path of your new destiny.

A favorite quote of mine suggests there are two ways to get to the top of an oak tree, by climbing it or sitting on an acorn. How committed are you to your hopes and dreams? How committed are you to you?

Whether you realize it or not, the probability of success is yours to determine. It's your choice, begin to climb, or find yourself a comfortable acorn. Either way, know that the choice is yours to make each and every day.

See you among the tree-tops – hopefully...

> When someone genuinely believes in you, there's virtually nothing that cannot be accomplished. The only question is; do you qualify?

Stay Within the Lines

Stay within the lines. That's the way our children are being conditioned today. Coloring books, with predefined subject matter and boundaries, seemingly are much more readily provided than blank paper, through which the possibilities would be constrained by only the young mind. Feedback offered to the developing minds is firmly rooted in societal paradigms, arguably grounding otherwise burgeoning minds with limitless capacities to soar. Why isn't the sun yellow, why isn't the sky blue—we challenge their creations. We impress upon them that it's important they learn to stay within the lines. In this way, literally and figuratively, our conditioning breeches unguarded consciousnesses and rings out loud and clear. Above all else, it's vital that they learn to effectively *fit* in with the pre-established perspectives and rules in the world around them. It's vital they learn it's not so good for them to challenge the paradigms of that world, even in an effort to find their own understanding and place. Most often it is suggested to children what to think and how they should see the world. (To this day, it still drives me crazy to ask a small child a question, and have the parent tell them exactly what they should say. But I'm digressing again.)

In school, children effectively learn not to think but to memorize. Usually, the child that can most accurately and completely regurgitate what the teacher says or the textbook reflects earns the accolades, earns more of the highly coveted gold stars. And while, at various stages, the reward evolves from gold stars to grades, and eventually from grades to the best jobs and the most opportunities, a good memory, ability to accurately reiterate what has already been said, or written, and, most important, the demonstrated ability to stay within the lines seemingly remain the attributes that matter most. In math, much emphasis is placed on whether the answer is correct and neat, while little attention is devoted to the creativity exhibited—in other words, how the answer was derived. In history, it is merely a question of what happened and when, not what the thinking and wider implications were, or how the absence of the person or event would have potentially changed the world. In English, things aren't much different with neatness, spelling, punctuation, and word count held in the highest regard. Lost in the mix is spirited evaluation of the writer's premise, the uniqueness of any ideas put forward and formal consideration as to whether anything meaningful has actually been said.

During my freshman year in English, for instance, I was amazed to find that mechanics and grammar were worth a combined 90 percent of each college essay, while style accounted for only the remaining 10 percent. Just think about it, at an institution charged with dispensing higher education and extensively developing the leaders for tomorrow, given the documented grading format, it was literally possible to write essays simply following the constructs, rules, and guidelines, not really say anything, and earn a collection of As. Even at that advanced point in my academics, what was seemingly most important was staying within the lines.

What's the harm, some might ask. Maybe it's this conditioning that fosters a seemingly ever diminished pool of self-sufficient, confident, aspiring, spirited, resolute, and willing resources in society who are capable of effectively taking on leadership roles. And more important, maybe it's this conditioning that's fostering a diminished quantity of people that understand what it truly means to live a fulfilled life.

Just consider that, from the initial point in life many of us can first comprehend the spoken word, and in an ongoing fashion throughout, development of and reliance on individual thought and expression are effectively discouraged and muted by parents, family, teachers, and society at large. What else can we expect? On an ongoing basis, there is little opportunity to escape that underlying, yet ever present, message. It's imperative to stay within the lines. Mindsets deeply rooted in such conditioning aren't exactly fertile spawning grounds for leadership-attribute growth. Without meaningful intervention over the long haul, even independent-minded, charismatic, imaginative, and wonderfully unique and expressive people will likely become marginalized, destined to matriculate, destined to become merely credulous, uninspired and uninspiring, approval-seeking shadows of their potential selves, content to allow others to define the path forward, never to question the appropriateness of the ever constraining lines. It's pretty scary, when you stop to think about it.

Luckily, even as a little tyke, I was never all that accepting of the whole "stay within the lines" mantra. Life seemed to be immensely more interesting and fulfilling when the superfluous boundaries were being challenged, when unfettered exploration of the possibilities was allowed to forge a new way. Luckily, I was fortunate enough to have had a few interventions along the way—"against the grain" at the core, these unorthodox people and educational excursions served to emphasize the importance of explored individuality and the vast potential therein. And the more that door was opened to me, the less relevance "stay within the lines" could possibly have for me. After all, my emerging governing perspective suggested that boundaries were how challenges commenced, not how they were supposed to conclude. In my mind, a stay-within-the-lines mentality was about 180 degrees south of the perspective and attitude needed to be a leading force, to make an impact, to be a mover and shaker.

In elementary school, a significant intervention point was the invitation, because of an IQ test score, to join the Academically Talented Program. For a few hours a week initially, then for one day a week in junior high, a few of us were privileged to spend time in an advanced educational environment with specially trained educators. We were exposed to new perspectives, new ideas, new logic, new cultures, new professions, and, most important, a new awareness of the degree of effect we could have. We were challenged to think freely about things, both the tangible and abstract. We were challenged to consider the possibilities, and to question things, especially the status quo. We were challenged to follow the paths of our interests, regardless of any obstacles, until our true calling made itself known. Last, but certainly not least, we were exposed to an unflinching belief that, individually, we could get wherever we wanted to be if we were willing to do the required work and refuse to allow anyone, especially ourselves, to stand in our way.

It's likely the impact from that program, in part, contributed to me deciding, out of the blue, that I should leave junior high early and gain admittance to the most academically challenging high school in the city. Never overly concerned about, or particularly driven by, others' opinions of my actions (in other words, never pressed about getting As), my transcript left a little to be desired from the high school's admission standards perspective. Undaunted by the odds and undeterred by the promise of formidable challenges, I pressed forward. Unimpressed by perspectives to the contrary, with appropriate effort, connections were made, the case was effectively presented, the necessary assistance was garnered, and I was welcomed into the freshman class.

Looking back, deciding to go to the highly selective high school was one of the best decisions I made. In no uncertain terms, Central taught me that I was supposed to have a vision, an effective voice, a strong constitution, and purpose. During those four years, among so many other things, I learned that my thoughts could only possibly matter if I were prepared to do something with them. During those four years, I learned that I could make a difference, that I could change the world.

These two interventions, as well as a few influential people I've encountered along the way, helped me establish a passionate, independent-minded, explorative, and competitive, push-the-envelope, never-say-die mentality that continues to motivate me to this day. Armed with this mentality, I may not always win, but I am always in the game. With this mentality, life simply isn't boring. Everyday, there is fascinating new territory to discover, and everywhere you turn, there's even more purpose.

There is a great scene in the movie *Million Dollar Baby* that comes to mind: Asked by a severely wounded apprentice to take steps to terminate an otherwise certain vegetative future, the protagonist finds himself deeply troubled that he ignored his initial instincts and agreed to help the young insistent student be put in harm's way. Interrupting the generous flow of pity spewing forth, his best friend questioned whether (paraphrasing) he had somehow failed to witness the incredible brilliance that is only possible when someone stares destiny in the face, takes on all obstacles, and rises to the top, doing exactly what he or she was meant to do. He continues (paraphrasing again) that the hospitalized student is actually fortunate, since so many people, although living much longer, live in an ordinary way and eventually die in an ordinary way, mopping a floor or going to a mundane job. They never choose their fate in life, and they don't get to choose it in death. Those people manage to live through each passing day and never come to know what it feels like to approach their destiny, to truly experience life.

How true.

When it's all said and done, life is supposed to be about having a voice, believing in something, believing in yourself, following your dreams, making something happen, taking that next chance, letting nothing hold you back, being willing to ask why or why not, blazing new paths, discovering purpose, and living life the way it was meant to be lived. And if our youths are to be granted any legitimate capacity to begin to crave such potential, any possibility of one day experiencing the awesome sense of achievement and pride triggered solely when a component of one's destiny is fulfilled, we need more emphasis on individuality, more inspiration, interest, imagination, questioning, awareness, wonder, and dreaming. What is very much needed is considerably less inducement for children to always follow in someone else's footsteps, to always opt for the safe and well-defined route, to never question popular wisdom, and to always ensure their feet remain firmly rooted on the ground. Over time, this mindset gravely shortchanges both their perspectives and their perceived possibilities in life, ultimately limiting their universe of potential future achievements. Just think about it, if the youth are condemned to strive to keep their feet firmly on the ground, how will they ever learn to soar?

As for me, because of my mindset, parents who allowed me to believe, the influence of a few well-placed people and interventions in my life, and the amazing sense of empowerment and fulfillment generated by achievements so far, I have no interest in intimately knowing a life that doesn't have the will to soar. Stay within the lines, you say? No problem. Well, would you look at that, I just happen to have my trusty eraser and all the necessary chalk to draw my own.

The Spark

Each and every single one of us
Have been given a magnificent spark,
A unique blessing from our creator,
A gift and purpose to make our mark

An incredible eternal energy within
Fueling each individual inner glow
The origin of our distinctive passion,
Power to change the world we know

But many choose to ignore the gift
When sadly they choose to refrain
From the spirit of their potential,
Instead content to simply maintain

Void of commitment, no zeal for life,
Mundane, the tasks absorbing each day
Uninspired, coping, the time passing by
With dreams and aspirations hidden away

The truth is each and every one of us
Were created with an extraordinary spark,
But waste the gift, ignore our purpose,
And condemn our very essence to the dark

Lucky You?

Over the years, from time to time, I've found myself the target of passing, benign-intended comments from loved ones and acquaintances alike such as, "Things are different for you," and, "Life always seems to work out for you." And, to be honest, more often than not, those comments to some extent irritated me. The implication seemed to be that the sun follows my every move, that by sheer chance, maybe even divine intervention, opportunities simply fell into my hands. From my perspective, the suggestion that I was lucky, that the laws of nature and circumstance were somehow more favorable for me was completely ridiculous. That was until I was introduced to a woman who taught me the meaning of luck.

Flipping through a Sunday night's cable-TV offerings, I happened upon an interesting news segment examining the concept of luck. The reporter introduced two women with similar demographics and backgrounds but with opposing responses to the question of whether each considered herself to be lucky.

The viewing audience was invited to make an initial guess which woman considered herself to be lucky. (It was pretty obvious to me, but more on that later.)

A doctor described three exercises to which the women were individually subjected. Each exercise was designed to examine the impact of contrasting perceptions of self on the resulting behaviors and projected outcomes. The exercises were as follows:

- Initially, each woman was asked the quantity of accurate guesses they would make concerning the suit color (red or black) of face-down playing cards. The doctor explained that the fact that the first woman guessed she would get 50 percent correct and the second woman guessed she would fair far better was telling. Seemingly, although faced with the same conditions, the first woman's inner voice told her she could only expect to be average. On the other hand, the second woman's inner voice assured her she could beat the house. While on any given initiative, either could be bested over the long run by facilitating enhanced motivation, interest, and effort, the more positive outlook over the long haul provides a significant advantage to the second woman. After all, if you feel better about what you are doing, most often, you are bound to accomplish more. In the first woman's case, how can her mind and body be expected to get excited about simply being average?

- In the second exercise, the women were individually presented with a choice between two metal puzzles. Each was instructed to select the solvable puzzle and solve it. The first woman chose one and briefly attempted to solve it before returning the puzzle to the table. Upon selecting the puzzle she believed to be solvable, the second woman, in the words of the doctor, "just about had to have the puzzle pried out of her hands." Not only did she have faith she had chosen the correct puzzle, she exhibited unyielding persistence in support of that belief. In this case, as it turns out, neither of the puzzles was actually solvable. However, by extending and enhancing her everyday efforts, this empowering magnitude of perseverance will considerably enhance the second woman's degree of success over the course of a lifetime. In other words, generally speaking, the longer you work at something, the greater the probability of eventual success.

- In the final test, the women were asked to determine the number of photographs in a newspaper. The first woman carefully tallied each image, and upon scanning the final page, declared a total of forty-two images. Separately, four or five pages into the same newspaper, the second woman asked whether she needed to continue. She, unlike the first, had spotted the specially placed newspaper ad, which indicated there was no need to continue counting because the total number of images was forty-two. The conclusion: the first woman likely gets so stressed and so consumed by the task, that she's not able to maintain an open and relaxed perspective. As a result, the second woman alone recognized the opportunity, equally available to both. This capability liberally exercised over the course of a lifetime affords the second woman significantly more opportunities for success.

Once dissected, the second woman's perspective of being lucky was apparently simply a derivative of:

- keeping herself in a positive, relaxed state of mind
- expecting the best of herself
- being dedicated enough to persevere
- being cognitive of the opportunities that present themselves along the way
- enjoying the enhanced odds and perspective that comes as a result

To state this more succinctly: "We should shoot for the moon, and if we miss at least we'll be among the stars."

In closing, the reporter asked the woman if she had always considered herself lucky, if she would still consider herself lucky if she fell and broke her leg the next day. With an almost contagious smile, she responded that would be the perfect opportunity for her to slow down, get some rest and accomplish a few important things she has been meaning to get done.

And it's that positive aurora, that air of confidence, that engaged persona that made her immediately identifiable as the lucky one. What she has apparently come to realize is if you truly want to be lucky in life, you can't simply wait around for luck. Truly lucky people have to stack life's deck in their favor with their attitude and their actions. They must believe they will win and always play accordingly, allowing improved odds to validate those expectations more often than not. They must, even in defeat, appreciate the challenge and eagerly anticipate the next challenge down the road.

Based on her responses and behaviors, the second woman has come to embody a similar mentality. Maintaining that perspective in spite of life's numerous detractors, obstacles, and full-blown pitfalls is what truly makes her lucky.

Watching the news segment, I realized I resembled the second woman's remarks and actions. As far back as I can remember, I've always endeavored to create my own opportunities with passionate beliefs, a positive perspective, and diligent, inspired efforts. So far, it has served me pretty well.

Therefore, by association, and much to my surprise, it's likely I too can be accurately described as lucky. Further, by extension, implications suggesting the existence of different laws of nature and circumstance for some actually have some merit, although not in the by chance vein suggested.

Things are different for me. And that's exactly the reality I endeavor to create each and every day. If the appearance from the outside is that opportunities simply come my way, my only response is, "I guess I'm just lucky that way."

Are you?

> The ultimate power is that to inspire, and there is no more vital or deserving beneficiary than self.

Mission 1

Tomorrow, take the time to smile and greet at least five people you would not have otherwise greeted—nothing extended, just a, "How are you? Have a great day!" Notice the effect it has on them and you. And have a great day!

Then Life Happened

Despite the best plans or the most well-intentioned efforts, the unexpected will occur. Issues will find us, we will be let down, the proverbial milk will be spilt, and sometimes we will be even pleasantly surprised. Life will be what we make of it. As a result, to get the most from these events, to produce optimal opportunities, happiness, and fulfillment, it is crucial that we foster and maintain an open, positive mindset every day—especially the days we intended to proceed one way, and then life happened.

Where I Needed to Be

After a long week at work and yet another broken promise to myself of an early departure, I had finally managed to pack up for what I expected to be a well-deserved, recuperative weekend. I made the familiar walk through the virtually vacated parking lot with my intended destination in site. Noting a cooler tilt in the evening air, I settled into my somewhat worn but comfortable seat and started up the ignition intent on the short detour that would result in a relaxing evening at home with movies and seafood. I buckled myself in and shifted into first gear, content that in just a matter of minutes, my long and trying week would be completely behind me.

But what was this? The battery light was flashing. *Okay, no problem.* When you drive a vehicle that is sixteen years old, you get accustomed to the occasional indicator light going on and off from time to time. Just out of the parking lot however, I noticed my inside lights were getting dimmer, and the radio wasn't picking up any stations. *Alright, change in plans—forget dinner and head straight for the mechanic, about five minutes away.*

Two hours later and things hadn't worked out at all as planned. There I was, sitting on the side of the road in a dark and heatless automobile. I'm guessing I made for some interesting conversation for the considerable tally of carloads taking turns rubbernecking in my direction as they waited for green. Nope, this was in no way what I had planned for my Friday evening.

And as I sat there, a little cold, tired, and needing to use the facilities, it dawned on me just how blessed I was. The car could have simply stalled on the busy highway I had just exited, and I could have been in an accident. Fortunately it didn't and I wasn't. I could have not had a cell phone, the means to arrange for a tow truck, or the funds to pay for the repair (assuming of course that I would eventually make it to the mechanic). The police officer did not have to stop and make sure I was okay and light safety flares, but he did. And, most important, the young man that happened to be walking pass didn't have to take time out to walk across the street to verify I was okay and help me push the car over to the side of the road, but he did. As he put it, he had seen too many bad things happen in his lifetime and wanted to make sure nothing happened to me. And, with a simple handshake and a, "You're welcome," he was off.

As I contemplated his unselfish deed, I wondered, *would I have done the same*? How often do I stop to help people in need? The truth was, not very often. What I really wished was for the ability to better demonstrate my gratitude for the concern and assistance he provided me. The more I thought about his deed, the less I thought about my predicament—and the more I wished I could somehow repay him.

My thoughts were interrupted by a somewhat disheveled man that approached the car. He wanted to know if I had a cell phone he could use to make a quick call. His story: he had been waiting to catch a bus, but a couple had just passed him by. It was likely that by the time he caught the next one, he would be too late to catch his connecting bus. Seemingly, this was merely the latest issue in what was apparently a terrible day. He had only bus fare and an un-cashed payroll check, which he offered as collateral while he utilized the phone.

Still not totally convinced of the situation, and concerned about conserving the weakening cell phone battery, I asked for the telephone number and made the call. Once answered, I asked the woman to hold and handed him the phone. Though I could only hear one side, the context of the conversation was obvious. She was upset because he was supposed to be home. He told her that it wasn't his fault, the buses had passed him by, and further, since he was unlikely to make his next connection, he would need to walk the rest of the way. He indicated he would do what he could, but she shouldn't expect him until sometime after midnight.

Listening to him, it struck me: This was how I would repay the assistance I had been blessed with earlier. I had the power to make a positive impact in his life, much as the young man had done in mine.

He closed his conversation with the fact that he was using the cell phone of a guy broken down on the road. He added that he was stranded, I was broken down, and we were both having bad days. He hung up and thanked me. I told him that his day had just gotten a little better and handed him money to take a taxi. He thanked me and went on his way.

Sitting back down in my car, I began to wonder whether I wasn't broken down on the side of that road, at that particular time, on that particular evening, for a reason. Perhaps the real purpose of me being there had less to do with my car battery, and a little more to do with the difference I could make. And while I have no true comprehension of the extent of the impact for the gentleman who borrowed my phone, neither does the young man who assisted me with my car. Without his actions, and my subsequent frame of mind, I would have likely been too focused on my own problems and not my ability to help someone else.

Eventually, the truck did show up for the tow, which lasted a couple minutes. By the time she picked me up, my better half had managed to adjust her tight schedule and amazingly already purchased the crabs, prior to the store closing.

Although it commenced a little later than expected, it turned into a crab and movie night after all.

Interestingly enough, when I think back on it now, having the car breakdown minutes from my destination, being cold for a couple of hours, and the tow truck being late barely graze my recollection of that evening's events. Instead, being helped by someone, helping someone, trusting that things would work out for the best, and being thankful for all the blessings bestowed are the thoughts that come to mind. And those are the thoughts that really matter.

Things didn't work out that night as I had planned. (I've heard it said: "If you ever want to make God smile, tell him your plans.") Because I was receptive to the opportunity that came my way, I learned a lesson and, I believe, served the true purpose for which I was intended that night. Further, because you are reading this passage, the purpose continues to be fulfilled.

It is said that it takes many steps to produce a beautiful flower. Sometimes, different hands plant the seed, water, nourish, and protect. And sometimes, some of the individuals involved in the process will never see the flower mature and bloom. However it is no less essential that their contributions are made. Perhaps what really matters in life is not how many flowers come from our efforts but how many seeds we plant. And since good has a way of instigating more good, it likely the rest will take care of itself.

That's what I learned the night my battery died.

If

If every day I can
Challenge an area of weakness
And enlighten a troubled mind

If every day I can
Shed the weight of a petty quarrel
And assist an individual in need

If every day I can
Love myself as well as my brother
And foster hope in the eyes of youth

Every day I can
Attain a little more of my destiny
Every day move a little closer to God

When Life Happens to You

I don't imagine you're the type that's ever found yourself wondering, *Why me*? I'm guessing there's never been either a significant event or set of circumstances in your life that's ever caused you to question if fate had it out for you or why, in the card game of life, you had been dealt such a lousy hand. Further, I'll bet you've never had the occasion to find yourself in a bit of a downward emotional or psychological spiral, deflated, devoid of energy and clear direction, maybe even feeling a little sorry for yourself. Okay, maybe one of these thoughts occurred at some point over the course of your lifetime, but just once or twice, right? Or could it be that, on a more regular basis than you care to admit, you feel just a little hopeless, feeling that the ups and downs of your life seem to have considerably more than your fair share of lows. Perhaps even, on occasion, you perceive yourself to be somewhat of a victim, quietly commiserating with yourself, *Why me, why do these things always happen to me?*

I had a conversation with a coworker in which he admitted a growing frustration over the duration of time it was taking the company to finalize organizational decisions associated with a merger. I reminded him that every indication had been given that all resources in our discipline were in great demand and would be retaining their jobs. I further reminded him that he had been recently assigned, as a "subject matter expert," to one of the most strategic and wide-reaching technology projects in the new company. His response was, "I know, I know. I was doing fine with things until a few days ago, but now I just keep worrying." I recounted for him a *Mad TV* skit I'd seen some time back that I thought was apropos to his situation.

A psychiatrist asked his new patient to tell him what issues had prompted her visit that day. The woman began to recite a litany of fears, worries, and phobias that severely constrained and, over time, narrowly defined the self-imposed boundaries of her every day. She wasn't able to do this. She was afraid of doing that. She was in desperate need of a means to begin to address the overwhelming psychological and emotional limitations that oppressively restricted her every move.

The doctor, listening intently the whole time, promised she was going to be glad she had come to see him because he was sure he could really help her turn her life around. He asked her to take out a pen and a piece of paper and to write down exactly what he said. He promised that, via three words, her life could significantly begin to change. She waited anxiously for the wisdom that she greatly hoped would permanently alter the path of her existence. The doctor dictated, "Just stop it!"

Appearing stunned, the woman retorted, "That's it? What do you mean? Don't you understand that I'm afraid to..."

"Just stop it."

"But I'm concerned that..."

"Just stop it."

"But I'm worried that..."

"Just stop it..."

I said to my coworker, "Even if the company took another six months to make a decision about the organizational structure, roles, and responsibilities, by my calculations that would equal about six more months of gainful employment for me." And given this and the fact that I happened to find myself in an enviable position, recognized as a key contributor on an incredible strategic project, the magnitude and relevance of which was not even viable before the merger, I was at a loss to find anything to be upset or frustrated about. I further offered that since his situation was not materially different from mine, he should, "Just stop it."

I concluded that instead of wasting time in the seemingly all-consuming, unproductive haze that many of our counterparts appeared to be spending their days in, perhaps his time would be better dedicated to striving to learn everything he could about the new technology. I assured him that was what I was planning to do. Until the time of the final decision, I committed to do everything I could to get well ahead of the curve. He agreed with the more productive approach and was off. When I saw him the next day, he appeared to have just a little more pep in his step.

Here's a thought: Suppose, contrary to his perceptions, the true source of frustration in my coworker's case wasn't actually the status of the merger, the timing of announcements, or determination of roles and responsibilities. Since none of these changed between our discussion and the next day's elevated state, it stands to reason that the true source of his frustration was something entirely internal. His perspective was all that changed, not any of the external causes he had held to blame. In effect, what the conversation yielded for him was that whether or not he would continue to feel helpless was entirely up to him. On the other hand, the power to wield meaningful influence not only over his attitude but the outcomes of the events in his life was completely within his hands.

What a powerful message.

Thinking about the brief conversation sometime afterward, it occurred to me that at the root of my coworker's changing perspective was a simple equation:

$$\frac{\text{Helplessness}}{\text{Time}} = \text{Hopelessness}$$

(Helplessness over time equals hopelessness.)

When individuals have come to perceive themselves as helpless regarding their ability to positively influence the status of a worsening situation, real or perceived, it's only a matter of time before the accompanying state of melancholy disintegrates into a growing state of hopelessness. A downward spiral is produced, which, unchecked, only grows progressively more corrosive to both the psyche and potential of those so afflicted. And worse, the afflicted never even come to realize they are.

At the other end of the spectrum, it is perfectly logical for someone who legitimately feels empowered and materially capable of defining, at least in part, their reality to feel energized, passionate, and substantially more optimistic about the future, regardless of the situation they find themselves in. These individuals never come to perceive their outcomes as a reflection of chance or some outside all-controlling force. They believe that the power to influence is always in their hands. This mentality creates a spiral of a completely different sort.

It stands to reason that individuals entrapped in the mentality of the former spiral tend not to be very happy people. Helplessness and hopelessness have a way of producing that effect. As for those immersed in the mentality of the latter spiral, these individuals tend to be considerably happier, more enthusiastic, and more fulfilled people. Put a different way, regardless of the situations encountered, people who perceive that they have options, people who believe they have the power to positively influence their outcome, can't help but live their lives with a little more pep in their step.

Just to be clear, in no way do I mean to suggest every problem is insignificant or imagined. The reality is that no matter the spiral of choice and no matter who we are or what we do, every once in a while, a serious issue is going to find us. Someway and somehow, every so often, life is going to manage to get a good punch in. Sometimes, the hand that happenstance deals us will be the worst at the table. From time to time, time will reveal that the people we chose to trust most deserved it the very least. Yes, the simple truth is that undesirable circumstances can and will find their way to our doorsteps. However, most especially in these instances, by virtue of our mindsets and by virtue of whether our spiral of choice finds us entrapped in helplessness or immersed in potential, the perspective employed, the manner in which we respond, the potential for growth, how effectively we ultimately choose to play the hand, and so our resulting outcome is up to each of us.

Whenever life happens to us, whether the resulting impact is big or small, our response is entirely within our control. Will we passively accept the role of victims or passionately endeavor to be the victors? Will we simply allow life to happen to us, convinced that our circumstances are synonymous with our fate, or will we respond with an attitude, and in a manner that causes us to happen to life?

Within each issue, from the most significant to the solely perceived, there is something to be learned, there is growth to be achieved, there is fulfillment to be found. When life presents us with tragedy, we must not only strive to survive it but to learn from it, psychologically and/or spiritually prosper from it and grow. When life presents us with our very own cone of choice on the hottest and most humid of days, we can frown and complain about the dripping substance quickly deteriorating into a sticky mess on our hands and clothes or we can smile like we haven't since we were kids and get to licking. As with practically everything else in life, our attitude is paramount, our response is self-fulfilling, and the choice is up to each of us.

Without a doubt, sooner or later, life will deliver the next punch. What will we do if it connects?

Simple Acts of Kindness

Two young women reading the newspaper
Discussed the contents with utter disdain,
They couldn't believe the loss of compassion,
They refused to accept the cycle of pain

So a pact was the result to make a difference
And in exactly a year's time return and explain
The vital impact each had made in the world,
Concrete reasoning their living was not in vain

Three hundred and sixty-five days to the day,
One's spirit and motivation had completely waned
She asserted I required more funding and support,
"There wasn't time for a difference," she complained

Because of my results the second woman offered,
My passion and energy requires effort to contain.
Within a week I had visited my ill grandmother,
Reached a teenager, and a man in cold and rain

"But our commitment was to change the world,"
The first interrupted, her anguish harder to retain,
Your deeds represent simple acts of kindness,
But to a world impact they simply do not pertain

"Convince my friend's daughter," was the response,
Angry with parents and rules she didn't entertain
Experimenting with drugs, sex, and a bad crowd,
I depicted the likely future, her way she's regain

Or the man I befriended looking for spare change
Due to a family feud vowed homeless he'd remain
I gave phone money and asked what he had to lose
Since someone told me he was back home again

And of course my visit to my grandmother's sick bed,
Short of time as a result of a tumor in her brain
My intent was to comfort her for possibly the last time
But surprisingly it was I who realized the gain

"This life is never long enough," she opened up to me,
"We're always searching for meaning we can't obtain
But the key is in simple acts of kindness for others
Those acts result in other acts allowing love to reign"

"So don't complain and think things can't get better,
And from limiting doubts or excuses always refrain
Everyday endeavor to practice simple acts of kindness
Benefactors will then practice, to complete the chain."

It was the last lesson she would ever teach me
And an integral part of me it will always remain,
Since that visit everyday I change the world a little
When I initiate another simple acts campaign

The two women agreed to meet in another year,
Both assured this time of success they would attain
Their goodbye however was cut off abruptly
They rushed off to help a man who'd dropped his cane

Attitude Adjustment

I woke up one morning to find that recently-planted flowers had been ripped from the garden bed and tossed on the driveway. The landscaping check had not even cleared my bank account and somebody with a discipline-deficient upbringing had had nothing better to do than pull an overnight juvenile prank. As I stood there reviewing the result, I realized I was at a fork in the road. I could let the culprits win by reacting in a negative fashion or I could assume control of my attitude, my response, and the outcome of my day.

So there, in my tie, suit pants, white shirt, and wing tips, I patiently replanted the dislodged flowers, carefully repacking the dirt and liberally watering them. You see, I realized that regardless of the fact that someone had nothing better to do that night (like sleep, for instance), no one else except me was in control of what kind of day I was going to have. As a result, I may have made it to work a little later than expected, but I had a terrific day.

A little something to remember the next time someone tries to rain on your parade. Because of them, on behalf of them, be sure to have a wonderful day!

> If you've never laid brick, can you ever fully appreciate the wall?

I Didn't Find What I Was Looking For

I didn't find what I was looking for. Those were the only words that comprised a recently received email concerning SomethingToShare.com. Despite the very much diverse offering of inspirational content and the non-existent cost of admission, it's peculiar that a tiny population of visitors have little to offer except negativity. It is customary for individuals of this type, armed with the minimal comprehension and shortsightedness of merely a few uncommitted clicks, to be perfectly willing to pass uninformed judgment.

I remember the initial, "I didn't find what I was looking for" response I ever received temporarily invoked feelings of concern and confusion. Not too long thereafter, I realized that being overly concerned with the tainted views of the few only served to devalue the heartfelt thoughts and praises of the many inspired visitors. And frankly, that wasn't an option that I found to be even remotely acceptable. Attempting to gain a little more insight into the mindset behind the most recent email and a sense of from whence this mentality originates, an interesting revelation occurred.

A few months earlier, I had heard a motivational speaker relate a story about a visit to the east coast. Upon meeting a woman familiar with his work, he found himself engaged in a friendly conversation. The woman asked whether west coast neighbors tended to be friendly. His response was, "Well, I don't know. Do you find people friendly on the east coast?"

"People here are terrific," replied the woman. "Neighbors look out for each other, people are generally pleasant, and it's a good place to live."

To which the motivational speaker suggested, "I think that's about what you would find on the west coast."

Later that day, he found himself in a similar discussion with another woman curious about his perspective. When asked whether he found California people to be friendly, he asked whether she found east coast people friendly.

"No, not really, people here don't seem to have much interest in each other. They don't talk much and they don't seem to have much to do with each other," she finished.

"Well, that's about what you'll find on the west coast," the motivational speaker offered in response.

How could his answer in both conversations be the same? To answer that question, we should first examine how two women, living in the same area, could have such completely opposite perspectives about their immediate environment. Could it be that their respective perceptions have little to do with the environment itself and considerably more to do with the overall perspectives of the individuals involved?

In the end, what we find in this life is primarily influenced by what we are looking for. If we are friendly and open ourselves up to people, people will be more likely to open up to us. If we believe we are going to have a good day, we greatly increase the probability. And if we look for the good in someone or something, that's exactly what we will most often find.

As our perspectives tend merely to be extensions of our most ardent paradigms, I realized the author of the email was in fact incorrect. In reality, he or she had found exactly what he or she was looking for; just as numerous positive-minded individuals have, prompting such inspired testimonials about the website. The website content didn't change, only who was reading it.

Essentially every day and every situation is ultimately a garbage in-garbage out scenario. What you get out of each situation is directly dependent on what you put into it, psychologically, physically, and spiritually. As a result, when the dust settles, the real message of the site, of life, is that inspiration can come, but only to those who would be inspired. Others will find only words and missed opportunity.

As each moment is what we make of it, I choose to forget about the one, focus on the many, conclude this particular passage, and enjoy the rest of this day.

Be inspired.

> Sometimes it's so hard to find the apparent logic because there isn't any.

Chasing Rainbows

A few years back, after a long work week and a drenching rainstorm, I found myself stuck in heavy traffic going nowhere fast. Although the likelihood was I would be late for my appointment, I reasoned that getting irritated wouldn't serve a meaningful purpose and wouldn't get me there any sooner. It was in that frame of mind that I saw it. It was a beautiful rainbow, majestically stretching across the horizon. It was a magnificent gift from above, which left me feeling extremely privileged and blessed, and pretty fortunate to be alive.

Then I began to wonder just how many of that afternoon's commuters even paused the hustle and bustle of their hectic lives to notice the glorious display. My guess is that the bulk of the motorists, especially those stuck in traffic with me, managed to miss it entirely. They were probably far too preoccupied with more pressing thoughts about the traffic jam, the time, the rain, the job, what's for dinner, the bills—far too preoccupied to be impacted by a simple gift from the Almighty. Because I was in a receptive mood, that incredible rainbow set the tone for the rest of my day. To this day, I can't seem to remember what appointment I was trying to make, but I warmly remember the impact of the rainbow.

What about you? Under similar circumstances, would you have noticed the rainbow?

There is beauty and magnificence around us everyday, however often we don't seem to be able to appreciate it. Every sunrise, every sunset, every tree with its rustling leaves, every soaring bird, every raindrop falling from the sky, every cool breeze, every cloud formation in the sky, the alluring scent of freshly blooming flowers, each and every rainbow bears magnificence, if we would only invest the time to experience them.

I have a question for you. What will it take to make you happy? I mean truly happy, not just happy enough for the occasional smile, and certainly not mere contentment that today wasn't that bad of a day. I'm talking about the kind of happiness that consistently lifts you to higher heights and can't help but positively influence those around you. I'm talking about the kind of happiness that, over time, can't help but foster fulfillment. Is that kind of happiness possible? Better yet, is that kind of happiness possible for *you*? Is it possible for you to significantly alter your path and your destiny? Is it possible for you to see life in a completely different way?

As you still are reading, it's a good bet that at least some of the questions were answered in the affirmative. My belief is not only are these concepts possible, it's what our lives were intended to be. Which leads to the all important question: how do we get there? It all starts and ends with our mindsets. To be truly happy, it is necessary to surround ourselves with a wealth of positive, inspiring experiences, people, and thoughts. In conjunction, it's important we ensure we are not so preoccupied with living that life, in effect, happens to pass us by.

Here are three vital steps that should help set us on our appropriate paths:

- Step 1: Adjust Your Filters

People often complain about the degree of negativity in the world. However, suppose it's not so much negativity as it is perspective. As it turns out, the information we choose to digest during the course of each day is paramount. Whether we realize it or not, countless times each day we choose the input we are open to receive. It's only natural that, because of the massive volume of data available, we routinely establish conscious and subconscious filters to efficiently manage the flow.

Not sold on it? Following are a couple of quick examples to highlight both the existence and effect of these filters.

The Existence: Try to close your eyes and just listen. Attempt to locate a sound that you didn't notice before. Try the same with your sense of smell. See if you can locate a fragrance that would have otherwise gone unnoticed. While the presence of these sounds and scents are unmistakable once identified, from the perspective of your consciousness, previously they didn't exist.

The Effect: (To get the impact of this example, complete Task 1 before reading Task 2.) Task 1: Take one minute, look around the room, and make a mental note of twenty items with blue in them. (Stop reading and complete Task 1.) Task 2: Now, without taking your eyes off this article, name twenty items in the room that have the color green in them.

The key isn't the number of items you could identify but simply the recognition of the existence of these filters and understanding the importance of managing them. By setting filters to emphasize certain environmental elements, we naturally de-emphasize others. As in the case of the rainbow, our filters must be adjusted to recognize, admire, and celebrate those simple things that are truly the essence of life.

- Step 2: Start a Positive-Thoughts Collection

Surround yourself with positive thoughts and words. Collect a few favorite passages and quotes that define the type of person you ideally aspire to be. Post them in the areas you frequent at home and work. Read them on a regular basis. Get in the habit of reading them when you wake up in the morning and quoting them as advice to friends. Amazingly enough, the more you think about them, the more they will become a part of you.

Endeavor to enhance your collection of positive thoughts as often as you can. Be on the lookout for positive, inspiring messages from wherever they may come. With your filters adjusted, you'll find positive input can come from just about anywhere—a movie, a book, a song, a loved one, a stranger on the street, even a memory.

In the movie *The Last Castle*, (a terrific movie), there's a defining scene when a military prison guard raises his arm to strike an inmate. The protagonist, a convicted three-star general and relatively recent addition to the prisoner population, grabs his arm, looks him in the eyes, and utters a simple yet powerful phrase: "You're better than this." Those words would prove to be both empowering and self-fulfilling throughout the remainder of the movie.

And as the sentiment proved to be empowering and self-fulfilling for the characters in the story, I began to consider the potential impact those words could have on my own actions. As a result, when I find myself in a mode that is less than constructive, regardless of the preceding circumstances, my resolve is to remind myself that I'm better than that. This triggers an immediate mind-state change and the implied necessity for me to live up to the sentiment. With minimal effort, even a simple movie phrase can become immensely uplifting and empowering in our lives.

- Step 3: Consider Your Sources

Last, but not least, surround yourself with positive people. Les Brown, a terrific motivational speaker, effectively expresses it this way: "Get the toxic people out of your life." In case you haven't figured it out yet, generally speaking, being in the prolonged presence of negative energy is both mentally and emotionally draining. And while inspired individuals with provoking, constructive thoughts are often difficult to find, the rewards are well worth the effort. A timely nugget of insight from an interested, motivated confidant with a positive state of mind can provide perspective, clarity, direction, and, most important, true inspiration.

With the elimination of most negative thoughts, occasional doses of positivity from members of your newly-formed network of inspired influences will offer unbelievable value. This coupled with the more inspired internal communication will serve to produce a much happier, healthier, more inspired, and infinitely more successful you.

In the end, it's important to understand that life boils down to a collection of self-fulfilling prophecies. When you wake up in the morning and anticipate you will have a good or bad day, chances are you will be correct. My theory is that the way we feel is about 15-20 percent circumstance and 80-85 percent perspective. If we alter our perspective, we can't help but change our lives. Or, to quote W. Mitchell (a highly recommended motivational speaker—his story will touch you): "It's not what happens to you, it's what you do about it that matters."

I'm reminded of a conversation with an unhappy and frustrated friend, whom I attempted to offer a little perspective. As much of her concerns were work related, I suggested that only she was responsible for her perspective, that her coworkers couldn't affect her state of mind without her concurrence. She asked me how it was that I always seemed happy. As an example, I offered that, although we were beginning a long, typically less-than-productive mandatory meeting, which my recent late work hours suggested I didn't have time for, I'd maintain a positive perspective via occasional outward glances to take in the rustling trees and beautiful sky. I indicated that at those times, although I would be at the meeting, I wouldn't be. I would be enjoying scenery that, without the meeting, I would never have seen. Her response was, "That's too simple. As a concept it makes sense, but it wouldn't work in real life."

My comment to her was, "If you want to keep getting what you're getting, you should most definitely keep doing what you're doing."

When it comes down to it, being happier is simply a matter of keeping yourself in the right state of mind and surrounding yourself with positive people and positive thoughts. Think about it: What is the happiest population of people we know? Young children. And what are happy young children surrounded by? Toys, laughter, and friends interested in the same. Young children are not just happy because they are young children. Like any adult, their mood is reflective of whether they have a nurturing, positive environment. Permanently remove the toys, laughter, and like-minded friends, and odds are that young child won't remain happy much longer.

In the final analysis, life doesn't just change on our behalf. We have to change it. While it takes effort, the dividends are well worth the investment. There's a story I heard once of a young man passing a porch where an older man sat in a rocking chair next to a moaning dog. The young man asks what is wrong with the dog. The older man responds that the dog is only moaning because he is lying on a nail. The young man further inquires why the dog doesn't just get up off the nail. The older man offers, "Well, I guess it's not hurting him that much, is it?" What about you? Are you lying on any nails these days? If you are, how much is the nail hurting you?

Make the investment in yourself. Change your filters, collect all the positive input you can, and eliminate the negative influences in your life. Believe me; it will do wonders not only for your perspective, but for the degree of passion that defines your life.

Take a little time out of your life to commit to this, and I'll catch you at the next rainbow.

Each Day

With each day I find myself changing
This life has become less simple now
The world around moves at a frantic pace
For me each day seems to slow down

I believed the answers were in my grasp
In those younger, innocent years gone by
I knew exactly what I wanted out of life
Conviction and dreams were in great supply

But something derailed me along the way
Something unexpected, far from sublime
My life is changing right before my eyes
I have begun to realize the passing of time

What was important has now lost significance
Like lofty ambitions that guided each day
My Christmas list grows shorter every year
My inner circle of friends seem further away

I care, but how much I'm not always certain
Indecision once was terrain I did not know
Now that's where I frequently find myself
Often now, faith determines my life's flow

As bleak as the picture seems sometimes
I must see the good things along the way
I remember happy is mostly perspective
The sun sets, I smile, soon comes a new day

No Forest, Only Countless Trees

While I wasn't particularly enthusiastic about attending yet another company-mandatory class, surprisingly, I found myself actually looking forward to participation in the afternoon's segment. Separated in various sized teams before the break based on our response to a question, we were informed that each team would be required to examine our thoughts and perspectives concerning everyday application of the morning's paradigm challenging theories and present the findings to the class. As it turned out, my group was by far the smallest, with merely one other member—a coworker I had not previously known. Little did I suspect that such a seemingly straightforward project would be littered with such cutting and pervasive personal issues, long-standing personal issues not yet resigned to resolution.

Upon commencement of the exercise, it didn't take long before reflections of highly-sensitive, deep-seated personal issues within my team member began to breach the surface. Her issues centered on a perceived lack of fairness, and the perception that the allotment of opportunities afforded her over the course of her career had been neither consistent nor comparable with others. It was obvious, by virtually every response she uttered, that deep resentment was present because she didn't feel she'd had the kind of resources and access she perceived others had enjoyed.

And by no means was this a recently-developed perspective. To the contrary, apparently years of unchallenged blame and contempt had, over time, given way to a toxic mix of anger and disdain, which was seemingly boring an ever-deeper hole into her psyche day by day. Little did she realize, it was all affecting her in ways she didn't even begin to comprehend, effectively robbing her of the very opportunities for which she so desperately yearned.

I reasoned, maybe I had managed to identify my true purpose for being in that class, on that day. As she seemed relatively intelligent, it was my belief that a more optimistic, inspiring mindset would foster new potential for her. And, given my position, I believed I could offer her some level of support in getting some additional doors open. I set out to introduce a new perspective. I endeavored to have her consider the thought that attitude is everything, and without a positive attitude, it becomes difficult to see even the opportunities immediately around us. I attempted to have her consider the possibility that the opportunity and visibility she so desperately sought could be directly before her, as attainable as impressing one of the various managers in the class, soon to be fixated on our presentation.

This all made perfect sense, right? The power to attain the very opportunities she harbored so much resentment about was being put squarely within her reach. The message was simple: *If you condition yourself to always look for the bad, it becomes pretty difficult to see the good.* The reality was she had gotten a good education along the way, and had obviously been afforded enough opportunities to be in a good job at a good company, a job that countless others of whatever persuasion would have been absolutely thrilled to have. Her attitude was not only causing other potential benefactors to stay away, it was also causing her not to see opportunities around her.

And she didn't have to take my word for it either. The presentation offered the perfect opportunity to put some of this new philosophy to the test. What did she have to lose? Simply commit to the presentation, avail herself of any opportunities that arose from me or any other manager in the class and proceed from there, right? The opportunity was hers.

How difficult would it be to simply try it, to seize this moment and expend the little energy necessary to part those dusty, heavy, psychological curtains long enough to let just a little sunlight have the chance to, at least temporarily, illuminate her psyche? The kind of opportunity she claimed to have wanted so much, and for so long, was potentially staring her in the face. Surely the potential reward was, at least, worth a try, right? Well, not exactly.

As it turned out, results were just the opposite. Every attempt to shed traces of light on the defenses of her heavily protected psyche with positive perspective was fended off with fierce resistance. Every inspiring thought became the victim of indiscriminate attack, fueled by disdain. Every bright light of opportunity was brutally decimated by a mindset irreparably tainted by the prolonged effects of unchecked anger and misallocated blame. Seemingly, years of this unchallenged pessimistic perspective had long ago constructed a monument of sorts. And there were no signs that immensely dense chip on her shoulder was going anywhere any time soon.

When the assignment commenced, I had every intention of extending whatever assistance I could offer that day and beyond. Given the response, the attitude, the blame, the distrust, and general overall pessimism, however, in a matter of minutes, I determined the problem was much bigger and more ingrained than my available time, energy, or inclination could withstand. And I couldn't help but wonder how many other concerned parties in her life had arrived at the same conclusion. I wondered how many missed opportunities there had been over the years. I wondered how many opportunities would be doomed to the same fate in her future.

When it's all said and done, the quality of one's life comes down to perspective. And at the end of the day, at the end of our lives, if our respective perspectives are positive, our time on this earth will be defined as such. Whatever our situations or circumstances in this life, without the presence of readily available, self-inspired optimism, without the ability to see the good, things can't help but seem significantly worse. Put another way, going through life without any sense of optimism is analogous to watching one of the old 3-D movies without the all-important 3-D glasses. We may be able to view the movie, but we truly miss out on all the special effects. It's no coincidence that the reviews for the movie were always strongest from the movie watchers equipped with the special glasses, by those who could actually experience, and fully appreciate the movie with all those amazing special effects.

The simple truth is; life is what we make of it. If we look for the good in things instead of the bad, that's what we will find, and vice versa. Maybe happiness and fulfillment begin with the simple act of focusing primarily on the positive and, as much as possible, letting everything else take care of itself. In other words, as so aptly suggested in the Bob Marley classic: "Don't worry about a thing, 'cause every little thing is gonna be alright."

Sesame Street, arguably responsible for the greatest children's programming ever, many years ago, had a regular segment: "That's About the Size." The camera would zoom tightly in on a subject and off camera kids, as well as at least some of the viewing audience, would attempt to guess what the subject was. Upon widening the view, the subject would become easily identifiable. To the amazement of all of us kids, we would find the bulk of our guesses completely off the mark. There would be some dialogue, followed by the jingle: "That's about the size, where you put your eyes, that's about the size of it."

Who knew, at the time, that we were being presented with the foundation for one of the most vital enablers for a happy and successful life? I wonder how much of that highly impressionable audience even subconsciously absorbed the empowering underlying message. I wonder how many times my assignment partner had viewed that *Sesame Street* segment during her years of impressionable youth; and if she had seen it, whether the underlying message ever came through that in order to see things clearly, to interpret things appropriately, we have to be able to continuously tweak our perspective. (Personally, I could have spent a lifetime convinced I was viewing a tree trunk, if they had not adjusted the view to reveal an elephant.)

In this life and in our outlook, perspective is everything. Either the positive things around us or the negative can consume the lion share of the lives we are to have and how we are to be defined. Whether we realize it or not, living negatively or positively is a choice that each and every one of us makes countless times during the course of each and every day. And the choices we make, whether consciously or subconsciously not only become habit but also designate the self-fulfilling prophecy that will guide us the remainder of our lives. As a result, it is vital we continuously tweak our perspectives, so more of the positive will be anticipated and seen, fostering more and more positive things to more frequently come our way.

Ultimately, there's some good news and some bad news. The good news is that you have the power to truly enhance your perspective in this life—you are in the driver seat for the real opportunities and generating the meaningful possibilities that come your way. The bad news is that only you have that power. So if you are not traveling in a positive direction, if you're not moving toward where you want to be, no one else can correct it. It is solely up to you.

In the final analysis, if we are to see the opportunities all around us, we have to be willing to open our eyes, minds, and hearts. However, sometimes to truly recognize them, as in the *Sesame Street* segment, it's necessary to step back a little and adjust our perspectives.

As for the young woman in the class, I was unsuccessful at influencing her at every turn, and so I gave up on the notion of making an impact, and delivered a thought-provoking, well-received presentation essentially on my own. Any intention to provide assistance subsequent to the class, to help foster additional options for her, was canned. What was the point of investing my time and effort? (I've heard you can take a horse to water, but you can't make him drink.) The young woman was far too deeply rooted and content in the house of blame and negativity she had managed to construct for herself. And there was no indication that her perspective had any chance of changing anytime soon.

I have not seen her in the years since the class. Truth be told, I wouldn't know her if I had. I can only hope, for her sake, that something happened, something eye-opening and life-changing so the fortification of her house isn't continuing. I can only hope that someone has helped her to realize that eventually, one way or the other, for his own sake, the stubborn horse must succumb to thirst. I can only hope someone has found a way to help her step back and realize that when you change your perspective, life's possibilities abound. I can only hope somehow she has come to realize that there's a lot more in this place to choose from, to concentrate on, to be excited about, to strive for, to believe in, to appreciate, to be defined by, to dedicate your time to, to be inspired by, to experience, to grow from, to be thankful for than just a few, far too familiar, gravely sun-deprived trees.

While the interaction seemingly had no influence on the young woman, perhaps the real purpose was more aptly intended to extend far beyond. What about you? How is your outlook these days? Has your perspective possibly become limited, and consequently self-defeating because of a fixation on a few overshadowing and otherwise inconsequential trees? Are you ready to step back, alter your perspective, and open yourself up to a new and empowering perspective and a lifetime of possibilities? Is there any interest in experiencing the remainder of this life's incredible forest? If so, open your mind and heart, open your eyes and ears, and let the discovery commence. Brace yourself though; an undiluted dose of the amazing potential your life was meant to have could be just a bit overwhelming at first.

Don't look now, but it seems the forest is starting to come into view. Happy foraging to you.

> Character, it's simple, either you have it or you're one of them.

Scars that Last

Scars, deep emotional ones
Damaging scars from the past
Limiting, always lingering
Shame, low esteem, tears that last

An angel, born beautiful
Dainty, innocent in every way
Pre-teen, developed, an uncle's pat
Something other than play

A young boy, struggling in school
Problems trying to read and write
Laughed at and called stupid
Accepts the label, gives up the fight

A lonely girl, attends a party
Desperate for a friend or two
Willing to do whatever it takes
Drugged, disrobed for all to view

A young man, full of promise
Needs his dad to lead the way
Finds abuse and neglect, changes,
Becomes an abuser one day

Scars, deep emotional ones
Damaging scars from the past
Limiting, always lingering
Shame, low esteem, tears that last

It could be your neighbor
Your loved one, a family friend
That needs help, compassion,
Ask, listen, and let the healing begin

Changed

Let me start out by saying, as of writing this, I do not have children of my own. On some levels I guess that makes me just about as qualified as at least some of the purported modern-day experts on the subject. To be perfectly honest, this is an article I felt I wasn't even qualified to write until a good friend, a mother of two, suggested I do so.

Turn on the news these days and you will likely catch a story on one of the following: teen violence, teen drop-out rates, teen runaways, babies having babies, teen drug use, underage drinking, or teen suicide. It's all enough to make you wonder, *What's wrong with these kids today*?

What's wrong? Lack of responsibility, fear, hope, respect, direction, work ethic, appreciation, innocence, love, concern, time, wonder, communication, discipline, and encouragement, to name a few. Walk through any mall or down any street and sooner or later you'll come across an adolescent blatantly ignoring his or her parent's instruction—in many cases, responding with what they will and will not do. Listen to preteens talking and too often you'll hear "that *#*>&" or "@$#^ them." Walk down the halls of a junior high school and you're likely to see very expensive sneakers, jackets, jewelry—the works. In some high schools, you'll find students wearing clothes and driving cars the teachers can't even afford.

What's wrong with these kids today anyway? In a word: us—the parents, grandparents, aunts, uncles, friends, neighbors, teachers, preachers, even the strangers on the street. At some point along the way, we've forgotten about many of the phrases we came to know as we were growing up. We forgot great behavior-altering passages such as, "a penny saved is a penny earned," "wait till your father gets home," "don't do as I do, do as I say do," "because I said so," "it takes a village to raise a child," "go get me your belt," "if your friends jump off a roof, are you going to jump off too?" and the ever popular, "do you want me to give you something to cry for?" We've forgotten the sincere, matter of fact look a mother has when she seriously utters the phrase: "I brought you into this world and I'll take you out of it."

For anyone who thinks these are harsh, for anyone questioning the appropriateness of these messages for children, and, most important, for anyone out there who has adopted one of those new age, better-educated, you-want-to-go–into-time-out, Doctor-Somebody approaches, I offer the following:

If you want to keep on getting what you're getting, keep on doing what you are doing!

I heard the likes of these and more from two loving parents, guided by good-old instinct and tradition. They didn't need a college degree in philosophy or childcare, or anyone else who had one. Between them I acquired healthy doses of love, respect, faith, encouragement, and, last but not least, fear. Yes, fear! I learned at a very early point in my childhood (and was reminded throughout) that there were consequences for my actions. I learned that whether the consequences were good or bad depended primarily on my choices. These lessons are the foundation for the adult I have become. Don't get me wrong, I did get my share of whippings. (After all, every child has an inherent need to test the boundaries from time to time.) But I can assure you that my older brother saw more leather than I did. Believe me, deterrence is a heck of a thing.

I just know there was a time when kids were allowed to be kids, forced to be when they forgot their place. There was a time decisions were made by a child's parents—"because I said so" was all the reason that was needed— and not finishing high school was not an option. There was a time when many of the issues we hear about on the nightly news were the exception and not the rule.

Thinking about all of this, I started to wonder, where was I the day things changed? Recently, however, I found myself watching one of the morning news programs. There was some specialist touting what was likely his best-selling book on teenagers entering high school. I listened intently as the anchorwoman and author discussed the difficulties of high-school life for teenagers today, their need to fit in and the difficulty for these teens in relating to their parents. I thought to myself then, and now ask you, doesn't that sound familiar, maybe like when each and every one of us entered high school? It seemed to me that if the anchorwoman and author had paused and thought about it for even a couple of seconds, they would have realized that each of them, their family members, and virtually everyone else they knew made it through high school just fine without the need for that author's book or any other how-to manual, for that matter.

When it's all said and done, maybe things haven't really changed so much after all. Maybe, just maybe, what has really changed is us.

> People and stocks are similar. While on any given day, for one, the returns may not be as expected, appreciable wealth is best realized when we invest meaningfully in a sensible, diversified manner.

Wandering

Uncertain of their purpose
With little hope for the future
The children suffer

Void of a solid foundation
No clear direction to follow
The children suffer

Too much seen at an early age
With too many choices to make
The children suffer

Never satisfied with what they have
Never learning how not to have
The children suffer

With no real fear in their hearts
And a lack of appreciation for life
The children suffer

With no one inspiring to look up to
No parental figure they want to be
The children suffer

Because we are weaker
The children suffer

And because they suffer
The children wander

The time has come to begin to
Ingrain the children with the same
Values, beliefs, hopes, and constraints
Our parents and guardians bestowed on us

Then, perhaps, they will wander no more

The Power to Change

Back (many, many years ago) when I was in high school, I was privileged enough to be the recipient of a simple yet amazingly empowering belief. We were taught that, as members of the top academic high school in the city, with its long-standing impeccable history and reputation we were special. We were taught that each and every one of us could change the world as long as we believed we could. What a powerful concept.

I bought into that message. Through college, through numerous stages of adulthood, it permeates every challenge I have faced, every temporary failure I have overcome, and every otherwise intimidating situation that has found its way into my path. No matter what comes along, not only do I have the power to overcome it, but with a little belief, ingenuity, and passion, it's possible I can even change the world in the process. What an empowering belief.

Looking back on high school now, I have a new appreciation for both the message and how special we were. We were not special so much because we had earned attendance at one of the most selective public schools in the state as because we were privileged to have received such an empowering foundation.

At times over the years, I've found myself wondering, what if everyone adopted the belief that they could, in their own personal and very unique way, change the world? How powerful would that be? And what would a world of that nature look like? In fact, I've come to believe we're here, for the opportunity to approach our true potential, to make our very own distinctive impact on the world. Big or small doesn't matter, as long as the impact is positive. There are no boundaries—just opportunity as far as the eye can see.

Still not convinced that this simple principle can truly make a difference? Think about it: If I didn't believe, you wouldn't be reading this passage now. But because you are experiencing it, we now have the opportunity to change the world.

Need more proof? Do something. Maybe spend a day complimenting others, encourage understanding where there was none, donate time to a good cause, help someone to grow, challenge a negative perception, create something that enhances the world, encourage someone in need, challenge yourself to be a better person, pass this message to loved ones and friends. The feeling you get in return will be all of the proof you need.

How does it feel to be so special? Good. Let's get going, a world awaits.

Mission 2

Tomorrow, take the time to do something for yourself, whether it's a call to a long-lost friend, a double-dip ice cream cone (that flavor you loved as a kid), a gift for yourself, or just a couple of moments of quiet reflection and spiritual refueling. Do something you wouldn't ordinarily do, enjoy it for all it's worth and know that you deserve it. And have a great day!

Perspective, It's Here Somewhere

We forfeit far too much of our lives in useless states of fear, worry, stress, discontent, and pessimism. No happiness and fulfillment there. We need to regularly be reminded of the importance of time, how it's spent, and who we spend it with, and be on the lookout for the countless positive messages, events, and people all around us. From these, the greatest opportunities are born. If we simply look, perspective, it's here somewhere.

Begin Anew

Have you ever wished you could begin anew
To experience the things you always wanted to
To make sure each day in someway you grew
To accomplish big things, and small ones too

To make a difference via things you would do
To positively impact lives of people you knew
To spend more time marveling the sky so blue
And less time worrying about your list to do

To ensure your faith becomes increasingly true
To verify each day a good memory you accrue
The great news is each day you can begin anew
But seize this day, another isn't promised to you

> Someone loves you. At the end of the day, what else really matters?

One Day

It is said that the most valuable real estate on earth can be found in cemeteries because it is there that, buried among all the remains, are all the ideas and opportunities not invested in or executed. All of the "should dos" and "one days" are forever at rest, never to see the light of day. "One day," they all said.

We are here for a purpose. And that purpose is more than just marking our time and getting through each daily routine until we have no more. We are here to make our very own individual marks on this world. We were put here to make a difference.

I heard a motivational speaker once ask an audience: "What is it that you want to do in this life, that you really, really have a passion for? What is it that merely thinking about it, and the possibilities, brings a smile to your face? What were you meant to do in this life?"

American Heritage defines destiny as, "the preordained or inevitable course of events, one's fate." Well, perhaps, as eloquently stated in the *Terminator* trilogy, "The future has not been written. There is no fate but what we make for ourselves."

So why are you here? What is your true purpose in life? What has your destiny been up to this point in your life? What should your destiny be? Are your answers to the two previous questions the same? If not, why not? What step, big or small, can you take today to change your direction? Whatever it is, start today.

Don't let "one day" happen to you.

Whether It Rains

Noting my neighbor was not dressed in work attire one morning, as I headed off to work, I wished him a great day. His response was to hunch his shoulders and say, "I don't know, it's supposed to rain this afternoon." The interchange left me wondering, during my short drive into the office, whether happiness for some was truly dependent on something as random and uncontrollable as the weather.

Are some of us incapable of having a great day when the sun isn't visible? Or is it simply our tendency to expect to have a bad day, and even communicate the anticipation of such, resulting in the initiation of our very own self-fulfilling prophecy. How is it that we would even think about assigning something as important as our happiness, on any given day, or throughout the course of our lives even, to such irrelevant, unimportant, unrelated happenstance-based factors that occur during the course of our days? How can factors such as whether we wake up on time, whether someone cuts us off while driving, negative comments from a coworker or loved one, whether the day happens to be a Monday or Friday, or whether it's raining outside be allowed to affect and otherwise control our outlook, attitude, and perspective on a regular basis?

At various points in our lives, to varying degrees, virtually every one of us has allowed these random factors to govern the extent to which we perceive we can be happy and fulfilled. Over time, reality usually maps closely back to our expectant perceptions and impressions, whether we expect good or bad. In other words, if, in fact, my neighbor had had a bad day on his day off, the likelihood is it had considerably more to do with his outlook, expectations, his comment that morning, and any other limiting thoughts and comments expressed, and very little to do with whether any precipitation managed to cascade from the sky. There is no one, no thing, and no event that can, in and of itself, cause you to have a bad day with one notable exception: you.

Just a little to think about the next time you're sitting in traffic, after leaving late on a Monday morning, when you happen to see a rain cloud just ahead.

> Some of the best memories are the ones that have yet to happen. When they come, experience and enjoy them for everything they are. For it's a pretty good bet that they won't come this way again.

Yet Another Birthday

As I woke this particularly special morning to start my day, I decided to indulge myself with a little music to set the appropriate birthday mood. My choice was a favorite CD—a mix of oldies, reminiscent jewels instrumental to my years of youth. As one particular song began to play, it immediately commanded my attention. My reaction was of no surprise as it was one of my all-time favorites through a good portion of my formative years.

My mind began an unscheduled detour, the words, melody, and associated memories easily overtaking all other early morning thoughts. As a result, I interrupted the writing I had been immersed in and decided to rest my pen. For a few minutes, writing would need to take a back seat. Instead, I gave into the mood that suggested I lay my head back on my pillow. Yes, the collection of moments to come would most certainly get their just due. And why not, this was to be a day of appreciation. Refocused, I began to pay the much revered song its befitting homage.

However, as the song began to wind down, a thought, initially unsettling, made its way to the forefront of my mind. I wondered, how many more times, in my life, was I destined to hear this favorite song, rich with memories from countless days gone by. I wondered how many times I would hear each of my favorite songs before I close my eyes and the words and the melody could be heard no more. What, I wondered, would be the count? Would it be 20, 50, 100, or 500? Would it be 10? An interesting thought to have on the morning of my birthday, huh?

I recall and recount this epiphany not to depress. To that point, even as I celebrated the passing of yet another year, the thought did not, in any way, culminate in me feeling depressed. Instead, I found myself even more grateful, grateful for the time I've been fortunate enough to have, grateful for the renewed recognition of just how finite our time really is. As a result, there was, and is, a greater appreciation for the significance of the remaining days, with whom they will be spent and the nature and relevance of how I will choose to spend each day to come.

A revived commitment was made to be conscious of the fact that time is ultimately what we make of it—and that whatever we make of it, the clock doesn't stop ticking. This mindset suggests it is incumbent on me to strive to make the best of my time each and every day. This mindset suggests the same is true for you. It's incumbent for each of us to do even more of the things we consider to be favorites, to spend even more time with those favorite people, to listen to even more of those favorite songs, just about as often as possible. And when we experience those things, it's incumbent on us to enjoy, I mean truly enjoy, each and every moment for the absolute blessing that it is.

With the last note of the song trailing off in the distance, I was eternally thankful for the additional perspective the realization brought me. To my thinking, it was an incredible gift I accepted from above. And so motivated, I contently stretched and smiled. I vowed to, with baited breath, anticipate whatever new experiences and accompanying wisdom this latest milestone would bring me.

With an even greater sense of enthusiasm, I now await my next song.

> The gift of a little peace and quiet is the best gift you can give yourself, indulge.

Little Billie Syndrome

Life is not meant to be spent in the bleachers. Instead, living is about being part of the game. Living, truly living, entails empowering behaviors like challenging yourself, just doing it, taking a chance, having an opinion, and stepping up to the plate when the crowd is against you. How many times in life do we have a view and fail to express it? How many times could we potentially make the difference, only to talk ourselves out of it? How many times do we convince ourselves that our ideas and opinions simply aren't good enough and wouldn't be of interest to others? How many times do we avoid the opportunity to contribute a voice to the outcome for fear that we might say the wrong thing? How many times will we allow avoidance to define not only today's reality but tomorrow's potential?

I'm reminded of a humorous antidote I came across some time back:

Little Billie had managed to make it all the way to the age of six and a half without ever uttering a word. The doctors could find nothing wrong with him, and employed the parents to keep working with him until a breakthrough came to pass. One summer day, his mother, as she'd done in so many instances prior, gave him a sandwich and juice for his early afternoon lunch. Walking away from the table, she was startled to hear the words, "This sandwich is dry." Rushing back to the table with tears forming in her eyes, she cheerfully cried, "Billie, you spoke, I can't believe it, after all this time, and your first words were a complaint about your sandwich!!!???"

Billie responded, "Well, up to this point, things have been pretty good."

The story ends there, but I can't help wondering what Billie's mom did next. Well, suffice it to say, I believe I have a pretty good idea how my mom would have responded at that instant.

More to the point however, don't we regularly fail to compliment and support the good in favor of pending complaints about the next problem, at least until we manage to lose the good thing—upon which we take license to complain about our undeserved lost?

What does it cost to say what you think, to have an opinion, to engage in the topic at hand, to be engaged with the relevant things happening around you? Once, while on summer break from college, an inquisitive nine-year-old requested I teach her some Spanish. I confessed that honestly I hadn't really retained a lot of Spanish from the many classes I'd taken back in high school. Somewhat dejected, she gazed at me and responded, "I don't understand; if you had to be there anyway, why didn't you just learn?" It was one of the few times in my life that I've found myself completely speechless.

So, in that same vain, I ask you, if you are going to be here anyway, why not truly live?

> From this day, may love and happiness reign.

Back to Normal

We have to get back to normal. That was the popular sentiment. From the president to the self-proclaimed grief and terrorism "experts," everyone seemed to concur that the most effective way to respond to the horrific events of 11 September 2001 was to simply get back to normal.

On 9/11, America suffered a tragedy of few, if any, parallels. In a well-organized plot, terrorists transformed four hijacked commercial planes into fuel-filled, flying weapons of mass destruction. The aftermath—over three thousand deaths, untold injuries, and emotional impact, two 110-story World-Trade-Center towers completely demolished, massive damage to the Pentagon, mass fear, mass anger, declarations of war, a shaken economy, altered lifestyles, a shaken America.

The days after the tragedy saw astonishment give way to sorrow, then anger, then national pride, then a sense of determination. And that steadfast determination could be heard just about everywhere—via the airwaves, from neighbors, from coworkers, from strangers on the street, "We can't let this act change our lives, we have to get back to normal".

We have to get back to normal.

I still remember that Tuesday like it was yesterday. What I remember is that as the tragic events of the day unfolded, somewhere between disbelief and grief, something else happened. Our priorities changed. Work became significantly less important. People called family and friends just to check on them—to let them know they were loved. People went home that day and talked with their children. People hugged (I mean really hugged) their loved ones.

In the days immediately following, people canceled unnecessary business trips. Families spent more time at home together. Church pews were occupied like so many years ago. Firefighters and policemen were warmly recognized and hailed as heroes. Collectively, we slowed down and focused on the truly meaningful. We argued less and thought about people and their feelings more. Seemingly, we discovered just a taste of the way things used to be, what our grandparents, and their grandparents, knew as "normal."

Maybe life's trials and tribulations are supposed to have purpose. What if these events exist primarily for the purpose of presenting us with the opportunity of choice?

In response to these events we can choose to grow—or not. We can choose to search for deeper meaning, to gain a little more perspective—or not. We can choose to take note of and appreciate the countless blessings and people that enter and touch our lives—or not. We can choose to be open to the purpose and opportunities for psychological and spiritual growth presented by events that happen in our lives—or not. We can choose to slow down, to spend more time on the truly important and purposeful things in life—or not. We can choose to be inspired, to strive to make a difference in the world around us—or not. We can choose to work less and play more—or not. We can choose to strengthen our faith and our compassion. While choosing not to forget, we can choose to channel our energy in a positive fashion. We can choose to grow.

Merely months later, it seemed our shift back was complete. And why not? Our memories tend to be of the short-term variety. Typically, we've been conditioned to, when we experience pain, declare that we're past it, effectively put it out of our minds and hastily get back to normal. As a result, we forfeit our opportunity to grow.

One incredible story from September 11 is that of a young lady in her early thirties, working in the

World Trade Center that fateful morning. Upon feeling the impact of the plane striking the structure, she left her desk intending to vacate the building. While making her descent down the stairwell along with others, an announcement came over the intercom. The damaged area had been secured and everyone could return to their offices. Ignoring both the announcement and countless others changing their direction, she listened only to the inner feeling telling her to get out. At about the fourth floor she felt a rumbling. (What she felt was what we could only watch in horror on live television.) The building collapsed around her, and all she could do was ride the falling mass to the ground.

In darkness, in complete and eerie silence she found herself, buried in the debris that was, only seconds before, the world-renowned 110-story World Trade Center building, south.

With a heavy object preventing movement of her lower body and no light or sound to speak of, she could only yell for help. Those calls went unheeded. By the next afternoon she was losing hope that she would ever make it out alive. She prayed, asking God for a sign, anything that could offer her hope, anything that would give her the will to go on.

A short while later the sound of tapping cut through the darkness. She called out, someone responded. She managed to wiggle her hand through the debris above and a firefighter grabbed it. She was the last person to be rescued from the catastrophic scene.

Watching the still-somewhat physically and emotionally shaken young woman tell her story from her hospital bed a couple months later, a tear made its way from my eye. As the young lady thanked God for blessing her through a mixture of smiles and tears, I found myself wondering to what degree her life had changed. I wondered whether she was concerned about getting back to normal. I wondered whether normal had taken on a whole new meaning in her life.

In the weeks following the tragedy, our collective anxiety and shaken sense of security caused us to pause and re-evaluate our daily activities. Our pace slowed, our priorities shifted, loved ones knew they were loved, heroes were found in our midst, the simple things in life, the relevant things like family, compassion, trust, safety, sacrifice, time, and love became a little more important. Our priorities were in order. Home, once again, became the place where our hearts were.

Unfortunately, time doesn't complement a short attention span. Since the tragedy, we've managed to regress back to our September 10 perspectives. Importance has again been superseded by urgency, home has again been superseded by work, reflection has again been superseded by trivial pursuits. We no longer speak to strangers on the street. We no longer hug (I mean really hug) loved ones. Our heroes again spend the bulk of their time in stadiums and arenas. Time is again something we find on a watch.

While most other voices have long since quieted, I continue to call for us to get back to normal. But it's not the normal of today, or of September 10, for which we should be striving—it's the normal our great-great-grandparents knew, the normal we were collectively well on our way to knowing in the latter part of September 2001.

That's the way I would prefer to live my life, and that's the kind of world I would prefer to live in. What about you?

> Patience. It can't be taught, but it most definitely can be learned.

Winners and Losers

Why do we tend to concentrate on the negative and spend so little time on the positive? Why don't we find reason to celebrate more and commiserate less? Why, seemingly, are 90 percent of lead news stories covering some combination of ill will, disaster, and misfortune? Why does misery love company? Why is the group of people who are willing to slow down and gawk at an accident so much larger than the group that will stop to offer assistance?

I have a theory.

Sometime early on in life, it seems we unknowingly come to perceive success as relative. Somehow, otherwise perfectly definitive concepts like achievement, progress, good fortune, and accomplishment become not so absolute. As such, we become conditioned to believe the true value of these acts of preferment can only be effectively comprehended in comparison with the results of others. At some point in our lives, we subconsciously come to believe that doing well is only half the battle. The critical question becomes, are we better off than those around us? This perspective, once adopted, becomes the foundation of a life-long competitive spirit.

During our formative years, we come to understand it is not important whether the race produced everyone's personal best but who came in first, who is most popular, who earned the teacher's gold star. Acceptance becomes increasingly important. Inappropriately, we come to believe that success is most meaningful when it is validated and acknowledged by others. Eventually, we graduate from gold stars, awards, and trophies to job titles, ever-bigger houses, more expensive cars, all prominently displayed to bear witness to the relative value of our efforts, of our being.

I had a discussion with a six-year-old some time back about why she had been running in the street. She informed me that each morning the kids raced to the bus stop and she really wanted to be first. I asked why it was so important, and she responded (with tears in her eyes), "I never finish the race first."

I asked what she would get for finishing first. With that, her expression and mood dramatically changed as she realized, "Nothing."

Don't get me wrong, sometimes life calls for a competitive spirit. Sometimes it's perfectly necessary to match your skills and wits against others with the opportunity for meaningful reward. It's the other 95 percent of the time that we need to reconsider.

Why does misery love company? If my theory is correct, the mentality is: if you are doing badly, by definition, I'm doing that much better. It's the reason all the carnage gets the ratings for the nightly news, it's the reason for the popularity of many of the talk shows.

Parents, family, the educational system, and society as a whole serve to nurture this mentality beginning early in a child's developmental stages. It's not good enough to know that the child talked or walked. We need to know whether they did it at a pace that bested other toddlers. Before long, the child is actively competing with siblings and other children for the admiration of parents and others alike. Eventually, the child steps up to kindergarten and grade school where the quest can commence for the teacher's gold star. Whether through grading curves, spelling bees, science fairs, school fundraisers, organized athletics, each child gets his or her turn to be indoctrinated into the concept of "winners and losers." Quickly realizing that the pain of losing occurs considerably more frequently than the pleasure of winning and mimicking the adults around them, the child determines the most effective way to be a winner is to ensure others lose.

In other words, misery doesn't really even like company—it just wants to know that someone else is doing even worse.

Both the existence and impact of a lifetime of this conditioning was made painfully obvious to me in a simple game introduced in a company class a few years ago. The instructor asked for two volunteers. A young woman and I made our way to the front of the classroom. We were seated in chairs, back to back, and told we were not allowed to converse with each other. With a bit of a smirk on her face, the instructor explained that the game was called "Auction." She continued that the two of us would alternately bid on coins—a penny, a dime, and a quarter. At the end of the first round, we would settle up with the instructor with our own money to complete the transaction. Two additional rounds would be played after ours. She concluded, indicating that she would explain the objective of the game after all three rounds.

So there I was, my competitive juices flowing, sitting back to back with this person I did not know. My mind was racing. Somehow, I told myself, I was going to figure out the objective of the game and win. I had a lot to think about as I tried to determine whether there were any clues in the instructor's seemingly meaningless chatter. The instructor was going from one of us to the other, extolling the greatness of the penny up for auction, securing from each of us our latest bid. I decided that until I figured out how to win the game, I would at least ensure that I was beating my opponent. I decided I should walk away with no less than two of the coins. With each coin the competitive spirit seemed to grow. By the end of the first mentally-exhausting round, I had yet to figure out the objective of the game. I had bid highest for the penny and the quarter, settling up with the instructor to the tune of about $1.56. My opponent then settled up for her newly acquired dime and we were asked to return to our seats.

Two new volunteers were selected for the second round. After receiving the same instructions, they found themselves on the hot seat. The second round ended with the participants each settling up with the instructor for a little less than the first round. And my guess is that they walked away scratching their heads as well. (About the only thing I had figured out to that point was that this was turning into a pretty profitable side venture for the instructor.)

The instructor indicated she was giving the class five minutes of discussion time before returning to kick off the final round. Via group discussion, we came to the conclusion that the objective of the game was related to a discussion held earlier in the day on finding win-win opportunities, and we decided on a suitable course of action. Upon her return, the instructor requested two volunteers for the last round. I again volunteered, joining a first timer in the front of the class.

The instructor began her now familiar build-up for the seemingly priceless penny she held in her hand. The young woman's opening bid was one cent. She then approached me, indicating she knew I could do better than that. "Not interested," was my response. After additional selling and coaxing, my response remained, "Not interested."

The instructor moved on to describing the incredible dime in her possession, indicating she expected us to do better than before. My opening bid: one penny. With no counter offer coming to the auctioneer, a reluctant "sold" was her only response. The magnificent quarter would suffer the same fate when I responded that the one-cent bid so far was too rich for my blood.

Between us we made a thirty-three cent profit. The moral is that truly winning has everything to do with intelligently determining the most advantageous course of action, and absolutely nothing to do with ensuring my opponent is a loser. In other words, approaching a situation with a win-win-centric mentality can foster the most advantageous results for everyone involved.

Interestingly enough, the instructor never referred to us as opponents. That was the label I derived. She merely indicated she needed two volunteers. It was a simple game with a powerful message. Work against each other and lose over two dollars collectively. Work with each other and split a thirty-three cent profit.

Further consideration of this simple lesson suggests the need for a re-evaluation of many of our deep-rooted, widely-accepted perspectives involving competition. It suggests that, similar to when I walked away with two of the coins from round one, sometimes we may think we are winning, but in actuality we are missing the whole point. It suggests that when we go into our familiar "winners and losers" mind set, we may actually lose regardless of whether we finish first or last.

Just a little something to think about the next time your competitive juices begin to flow, the next time you worry about how much someone else makes, the next time you think about keeping up with the Jones. Just a little something to think about the next time you set an example for the children in your midst.

> Integrity is the inevitable distinction between true winners and losers.

Another 9/11 Story: Mike and Pat's

11 September 2001. By all accounts this was a day of unforeseen death and destruction, a day incredible sorrow would make its acquaintance with many, a day when monumental religious and ethnic intolerance became justification for the unthinkable, a day when time stood still as we watched, fixated, perplexed, and questioning, was this really possible? Could anyone have such an utter disregard and disdain for human life? By all accounts, 9/11 was one of the darker days in the history of mankind. Well, by almost all accounts.

Every once in a while, life presents us with a different kind of reality, a set of circumstances that leave us thinking, *Wow, can that really be?* Every once in a while, we are presented with a set of circumstances that offer compelling circumstantial evidence that life is fundamentally more than an assortment of disconnected, un-orchestrated occurrences and random happenstances. Even more, every once in a while, when we least expect it, life's circumstances can cause an elevated path of existence to be illuminated—one that beckons us to desire, and to be, more.

Because in this life our existence matters most when our true potential is what we choose our destiny to be. In this life our relevance in the time that we do have is only meaningful if we overcome obstacles and doubts to master our circumstances. However, will we make the difference? When the time comes, will we choose to care?

On the surface, Mike appeared a typical, relatively understated, good–natured, and unassuming man who was simply trying to care and effectively provide for his family. In actuality, his worsening health yet enduring inspired mindset combined to make both him and his situation anything but typical. Mike's need for dialysis was becoming dangerously pressing. If his quiet search for a new kidney did not soon yield a viable prospect, odds were dire medical consequences would depict his unenviable fate.

To foster employment opportunities and continuous improvement, Mike enrolled in a self-development class. Arriving at class late one day, he felt compelled to explain the reason he had not been on time. The class was fixated as he explained his requirement for dialysis, generating countless questions concerning the dialysis process in general and the medical circumstances that had assumed a commanding focus in the course of Mike's daily existence. Perfectly willing to educate his fellow students, Mike openly addressed each question. Amazingly, by the end of the four-day class, one hundred previous strangers had joined ranks, each student pledging to engage at least five additional people, and request that they engage others, in an impassioned search for a suitable and willing kidney donor.

It wasn't long before Mike's story found its way to Pat. Mike's predicament struck a cord with Pat, and she knew she wanted to meet him. Shortly after putting a face and spirit with Mike's story, she asked him, "Listen, I'm O positive and you're O positive, why don't you make an unrealistic request of me?" She had to say it three times before Mike understood.

Testing was completed and Pat was found to be a suitable donor. A date was set for the operation: 11 September 2001. Mike is African American. Pat is Caucasian. Mike's faith is Christian. Pat's faith is Muslim. The operation turned out to be a complete success and both Pat and Mike are doing well.

11 September 2001. It was a day of tolerance. It was a day of life. It was a day of love after all.

> Sometimes we spend our lives worrying about not having all the answers, forgetting in the process that what life is really all about is the full, unadulterated experience of the questions.

Things Lost

So many things lost in life
The happiness
The security
The simplicity

So many things lost in life
The youth
The wonder
The honesty

So many things lost in life
The communication
The friendship
The love

Why, why must we continue to lose?
The choices

So many things lost in life

Meeting Time

My father is a stickler for time. Tell him that you will do something or be somewhere at a particular time, and on time he will be with watch in tow. I believe he perceives that as a notable strength. It's one of the reasons he struggles some weekends with me.

A good friend once told me, in her opinion; I didn't appreciate the importance of time. Now, upon receiving constructive criticism, especially from someone who cares, I purposely pause to take in the new perspective, to consider the possibility of accuracy and to what extent the comments could be beneficial. In this case there was no need. Without hesitation, I informed her she was completely off the mark. I contended that I have as big an appreciation and as much respect for the importance of time as anyone she would likely ever know. Maybe, I suggested, we had completely different perspectives of what the importance of time really meant. It's obvious to me my friend knew nothing of Moken time.

I was fortunate enough to catch a news story one evening concerning a nomadic group who've lived for hundreds of years off, and on, the coasts of Burma and Thailand, largely unadulterated and uninfluenced by modern society. The Moken spend approximately six months of each year living in mobile homes of the aquatic variety. They are more at home in the water than they are on land, with their very young learning to swim before they walk. The Moken have perfected lowering their heart rate, doubling the maximum time they can remain submerged, and can see twice as well once they are there.

The story discussed how their remarkable intuitiveness, their degree of oneness with nature, permitted them early awareness of the danger signs, allowing the Moken safe retreat from the wrath of a looming tsunami. While death, injury, and destruction swept through the region with a force not previously experienced, the Moken, much like the animals that survived unscathed, either escaped to higher ground, or headed for deeper waters. The difference between life and death, their ability to read nature's signs granted them a pass from the fury of the pending storm.

I found the group's ability to be so in tune with nature's warnings incredible. They were able to escape the massive tragedy not avoided by so many others around them, who were armed with the latest technology and know-how. What I found to be even more fascinating was the nature of the Moken way.

When a little boy greeted the reporter, the reporter requested the interpreter ask the little boy's age. "I don't know," was the response from the little boy and an elder in the group. It seems that, within the community, there is no concept of the tracking of time, no need to keep an ongoing tally of one's time on this earth. There is no equivalent in the Moken vocabulary for hello, no translation for goodbye. There is no discernable excitement upon seeing relatives. Instead, all commingle and integrate to form a perpetual community of shared and interwoven lives, purpose, and being. And there's no need for formalized salutations if all communal relationships are perpetual. Think about it: loved ones are here, they're not, they're here again. The reigning perspective is if they're not here, they will be. And there's no questioning when because that concept too does not exist in the Moken language.

By the definition employed by my friend, I guess it could be adamantly argued that the Moken do not possess the slightest inkling or appreciation of the importance of time. How could it be of value if they don't even track it? Perhaps, given their life and resulting perspective, they have come to understand that it's not the tracking of time that determines its value so much as the kind of life one lives in that time, the impact one makes, and what one gives back to the people and world around him or her, the oneness one shares with nature, their fellow man and woman, and the creator above. Perhaps the Moken have come to comprehend that assigning the highest possible value to time, in the end, is most predicated on the extent to which perspective, purpose, fulfillment, and appreciation is a mainstay in the time you have, that time really becomes meaningful not because you track it or fill it with as many things and places as possible but when it is dedicated to something or someone that really matters.

Thinking about the news story, I smiled as I paused to consider whether I don't have at least some minute traces of the Moken bloodline flowing, ever subtlety, through me. Their sense of time, their sense of relevance, their apparent penchant for slowing the world down a little, appreciating what they have, and simply taking life in for all it has to offer—these are all principles that I constantly endeavor to nurture within. Their serene yet purposeful lifestyle, their unassuming outlook, their appreciative mindset for the many blessings they've come to know are evidence of an evolved mentality to which I have spent my years aspiring.

Many times, coworkers are perplexed as to why I don't have a need to travel during vacations, and how I can function without my weekends being pre-planned with an assortment of things scheduled to do. For me, the very best days of all, the happiest and often the most meaningful, are the days when nothing in particular is required to be done, when the time can be filled with more relevant, more life-affirming pursuits rooted in purpose, self-actualization, inspiration, creativity, charity, appreciation of nature, personal fulfillment, and spiritual replenishment, days when nary a watch or to-do list, in my possession, will see the light of day.

So while I've managed to come to terms with the likelihood that I am not of Moken descent, I'm guessing they wouldn't mind if a western chapter, of sorts, were chartered. I started thinking, *what would membership in such a chapter take*? There would certainly be no dues required and definitely no litany of time-sensitive, scheduled meetings to attend. Membership would be unconditionally open to those who, at least occasionally, are prepared to commit to fundamental attitude and lifestyle changes, and incorporate those changes, serving to bring the world ever closer to the kind of timeless, serene, grateful, responsible, purposeful perspective reflected by the Moken way.

In the spirit of the Moken, the governing principles for this western chapter would be decidedly uncomplicated and rather forgiving, while adherence would be monitored completely by self. Simply stated, the credo would be: Whenever feasible, especially on weekends and vacation days, we must endeavor to simply enjoy ourselves, our life, nature, and the people around us. We must endeavor to achieve more of our intended purpose for being here, ever more mindful that our true destiny waits. To exhibit true appreciation for the time we have, we must be willing to slow ourselves down enough, at least on some days, to really savor it. On these days, we should endeavor to accomplish, grow, create, relax, refresh our spirits, contemplate, remember old times, dream, laugh, love, and, most of all, be thankful. And whatever happens from there, whenever it happens, happens.

Each of these instances will be Moken time, a working holiday when we dedicate time to purposeful pursuits while also taking time to celebrate each day for the absolute blessing that it is. This approach to our days will foster a new motivating perspective. The beauty and potential of life will, as a result, more readily be seen. In turn, greater opportunities for happiness and fulfillment will abound. A new attitude will challenge old mentality, as instead of a litany of accomplished tasks, the priority will become simply to derive the most value from the experiences in each Moken-time-filled day.

As for anything not accomplished, no worries. Our new perspective should remind us there's always tomorrow, unless there is no tomorrow, in which case, perhaps it was never meant to be. Further, when on Moken time, there can be no worry. After all, there is no concept of worry in Moken existence. Much the same as worry, I'm guessing there's no translation for "stress" and "frustration," as it's likely these are concepts they don't even begin to comprehend.

What about you? Are you interested in spending at least some portion of your time without worries, without stress, without frustration, taking time to marvel at nature's beauty, at the wonder that is each new, potentially incredible day? Are you interested in more appreciating, exploring, creating, growing, more positively perceiving, believing, and living a more purposeful existence to boot? That's just a slice of what it means to be on Moken time. And if you're prepared to make a few adjustments, if an occasional break from the stress of the rat race, the hustle and bustle, and the daily grind sounds like a desirable thing, if you can envision a life composed of at least a few less required tasks and just a few more meaningful pursuits, if you are ready to try to decrease your focus on what you want (which also does not have a translation in the Moken vocabulary) and depend a little more on what life has to offer, then simply take off that watch, put down that to-do list, open your heart and mind, listen to your soul, and go allow it to happen. Greater purpose, perspective and fulfillment, and a new appreciation of the importance of time awaits you.

The first and last ever meeting of the Moken Western Chapter, with an encouraging nod and a smile, I now bring to a close. The best of luck and much Moken time to you.

> Stress is nothing less than this life's express to the next. Whatever it takes, get off the train.

Growing Up

Where did all of the years go?
And how did our youth slip away?
Was I home sick in bed the day,
The focus became work, not play?

Well, we have to be grown-ups now.
Reordered priorities are the way.
Work must have its proper focus now because
There are lots of plans to make for Saturday.

> Perspective can be of no consequence to the individual who has come to relish the act of worrying.

Mission 3

Who is the most important person in your life? Who is the one you can most count on when the chips are down? Who is the person that best knows your heart? Whose love has stood the test of time? Who can make the smiles and the tears a little brighter? Who knows when something is wrong, regardless of what you say? Who is it? Does he or she know? When was the last time you told him or her? When was the last time you showed that person how much you appreciate who he or she is and what he or she has done for you? Whatever it takes let that person know what he or she means to you. Do something special for him or her, and then say, “Thank You.”

The Personal Touch

Our humanity endows us with the license to hope. And within that hope we can benefit from another's footsteps. We can be uplifted and enlightened by another. We can be there for a troubled soul in need. We can be touched by another's predicament. We can realize that we never have to be alone. By extending, accepting, and helping, we begin to comprehend the infinite possibilities of the personal touch.

To Grow

If flowers are to be vibrant
Feeding and watering will make them so
But another ingredient is needed
If a healthy child is to grow

It's a hug and an encouraging smile
When the lessons of life have me low
It's the push for me to expand my horizons
While trying not to let the concern show

It's discipline whenever I needed it
It's the tear-filled eyes whenever I have to go
It's the pride for all my accomplishments
Resulting in the world's most angelic glow

A lifetime of receiving these blessings
Is the way that I have truly come to know
Most importantly it is a mother's love
That causes a loving man from a healthy child,
To grow

A Need to Change

Throughout my teenage years I usually found myself toeing the line between being the good student who lived up to my parents' expectations, and not living down to my worst nightmare, being labeled un-cool. I well remember one such occasion, when my father and I were readying for a trip downtown. Realizing that my father was waiting for me, I hurried downstairs. As I headed toward the front door, my father interrupted my momentum, posing a question dripping with audible disdain.

"Where do you think you are going?"

"Aren't we going downtown?"

"You are not going anywhere with me dressed like that."

Well, there was certainly no need for explanation or further discussion. A change of attire would be in my immediate future, and there was absolutely no doubt about the infraction that had caused the agitation. I had been wearing a plain white t-shirt (also known as an undershirt). You see, in my neighborhood, it was common for the kids, particularly the cooler ones, to don a white t-shirt and head out to the park, around the neighborhood, wherever. I thought nothing of putting one on to go hang out on my block or to the park to play a little ball. I'd never had the occasion to wear one out in the presence of my father. And the precedence certainly wasn't about to be set on that day.

It wasn't so much the words that left such a lasting impression as it was the look, the visible, unavoidable expression of utter contempt and disdain. Just the same, I can remember thinking he was obviously too old and simply didn't understand. I guess that, at least from one teenager's perspective, made my father a square.

Well, many years have gone by. Today I am what some might consider a relatively successful man, well immersed in the corporate world. Needless to say, adjustments have occurred over the decades, countless many of which have long since been forgotten.

One adjustment never to be forgotten was purchasing my first pair of Wingtips, soon after getting my first full-time job. For the uninitiated, Wingtips are inflexible, heavy, conservative business footwear that leave a little bit to be desired in the style category. Highly symbolic of corporate America, typically, Wingtips are something of an acquired taste. Purchasing my first pair represented a major hurdle, perhaps because I believed them to be about the ugliest shoes for which a cow had ever been sacrificed. No, the thin stylish models that didn't hold up long, developing holes quickly as a result of extended wear and rainy days, now those were for me. And given the fact that I was just out of college and didn't have a car, believe me, I had my fair share of soggy-sock-bottom bus rides. Still, that didn't prevent me from window-shopping for the Wingtips on many occasions, only to leave the shoe stores empty-handed. Apparently, somewhere along the way, common sense and maturity won out, as I eventually submitted to the corporate image. Today, an integral component of my image, my Wingtips and I are virtually inseparable.

Looking back on that day with my father so many years ago, I have come to appreciate something. You see, what prompted this particular trip down memory lane was, as I was making my way back to my current rung on the corporate ladder one morning, Wingtips comfortably encasing my feet, I noticed a young man. As I approached a traffic light, he was standing there, waiting for the bus to take him to that morning's primary destination. In years, he appeared to be just a little older than I had been so many years ago. Not only was he wearing a plain white t-shirt but he completed the ensemble with a blue wave cap.

At that moment, it again became apparent to me just how blessed I am, just how blessed I've been. I was fortunate enough to have a father who was concerned enough, knew enough, and was enough of a force in my life to make it crystal clear my attire was unacceptable that day. I was fortunate because he, and others alike, made what I believed to be my business their business, seeing to it I presented myself in an appropriate way.

As I considered all of this, the young man, and the potential prospects that lay ahead, a simple yet fundamental realization, the product of my father's shared perspective emphasized by countless enlightening experiences over the years, made its way to the forefront of my mind. On that day so many years ago, my father wasn't so much a square as I was naive. Whether we like it or not, the image we have matters in this world. The way we carry ourselves, the mentality we have, the goals we set, the communication we have within, everything goes together to determine who we are and will be. From that, our very own personal self-fulfilling prophecies are born and nurtured.

Our personal self-fulfilling prophecy can be empowering and uplifting, suggesting that if we present ourselves appropriately, people will more likely see us as successful. If people see us as successful, they will see each of us as someone to be respected and looked up to. If we carry ourselves in an appropriate manner, we will more likely be perceived as individuals with manners and decency, in turn causing others to more likely treat us the same way. Because others treat us that way, greater and more numerous opportunities will be fostered. Because those opportunities are fostered, our respective immediate futures will yield enhanced choices. Knowing ourselves will facilitate our making the best choices. Making the best choices will bring optimal success.

Both empowering and uplifting, that's an incredibly powerful self-fulfilling prophecy to have. But, unfortunately for the young man at the bus stop and countless others not yet fortunate enough to have gotten the message effectively ingrained in me over the years, the harsh reality is, it's not very likely you're going to get *there* when your starting point is a t-shirt and a wave cap.

What I now understand is that day was a turning point in my life. My father didn't explain all of this on that day. He didn't need to. For it to really sink in, I had to get it for myself. His responsibility was to plant the thought. His responsibility was not to let me out of the house dressed that way. It was up to me, open mindedness, years of living and experienced results to have it really take root and grow. The good news is I did change, not only my attire for our trip downtown but also so many other things since that day.

My suspicion is, the young man I saw during my drive that morning had no one back home to provide that kind of feedback, to prevent him from leaving the house that way. He had no idea that the t-shirt and wave cap likely gave birth to a completely different self-fulfilling prophecy as a result of the perceptions of many of the people encountered that day. My hope is that young man, and today's youth in general, will begin to be stopped at the door, that they will get that message before it's too late. Their only real hope is responsible adults like the ones many of us had growing up.

Know any?

Barbara's Story

On my short ride to work one morning, I turned on the radio just in time to hear a listener call in to weigh in on that morning's topic, which was the existence of soul mates. The woman committed that she knew without a doubt from personal experience that soul mates existed because she had found and lost hers. Recounting her story, she told of accompanying her sister on a trip to the hospital to visit the brother of her sister's boyfriend. She walked into the room to find him in the hospital bed with his arm in a cast. Though the only words to pass between them that day were matching "hi's," the exchange was accompanied by a chill that shot through her body. Carrying the feeling that there was something really special about this chance meeting the following day, she was surprised to receive word from her sister that he was also struck by her, and really wanted to see her again.

From the first date, it was obvious that they were meant for each other. Each kiss brought fireworks. The more time they spent together, the closer they became. After dating for a few months, they were each convinced they had found their true match. Then they lost each other.

A few months into the relationship her ex-boyfriend became a problem. After threats and an attempt at running the two of them off the road, the ex-boyfriend physically attacked her soul mate. Fearing any additional trouble or further harm to the man she loved, she cut off the relationship. A few months later, feeling terrible about what happened and terribly missing what she had, she contacted him to explain. His response was that he was disappointed that she didn't have more faith in him and his ability to handle the situation, to take care of her. They lost contact.

Sometime later she met another man ten years her senior. He was a nice guy who went out of his way to do things for her, to show her he cared. She fell in love with him, married him, and they have a beautiful daughter together.

But everyday, in spite of loving her husband, she thinks about her soul mate and the closeness and passion they'd shared. The two of them have re-established contact as friends. They both concur that things should have been different, that they should have been together. Her husband is fully aware of the history between the two of them and knows that if it wasn't for her commitment to their family and her soul mate being married, she would go back to him in a heartbeat.

After re-establishing contact, she discovered that the two of them had purchased a house on the same day and that each of them had daughters born on the same day of the same year. She concluded that every time she thinks of him and the feelings they shared together she knows that soul mates exist.

It was about this time, as I turned into the parking lot, that the show-host ended the call, opening the lines up for comments. The first call in was a listener voicing the opinion that the previous caller was crazy. How could she love two people? How could she tell her husband? And her husband must be crazy if he knew all of this and continued to stay with her. The other morning-show personalities chimed in that her story only further confirmed their beliefs that soul mates could not exist. And there I was with a tear in my eye (I'm a sucker for touching stories), saying to the radio, "You are missing the whole point."

True fulfillment in life comes from the belief, the hope, the longing for something special, something that awakens your soul and injects it with a healthy dose of passion. Believing in and caring about her story not only awakens a vital part of us, it gives us so much more to look forward to.

Thanks for your story Barbara. I believe.

> Real love planted in honesty, nourished with communication, and watered with appreciation will surely blossom.

No Laughing Matter

My better half has never particularly liked being tickled. After a bit of a hiatus, some time back, her feelings about the matter resurfaced again as a major point of contention.

While playing around, I made the apparently grave mistake of tickling her. In response to the cold reaction received from her, my mood took a 180-degree turn.

"I'm tired and you know I don't like to be tickled."

"You don't have to worry about it happening again."

With that, the tone for the rest of the evening was set.

Thinking about the argument the next day, I found the situation puzzling. It seemed to me that tickling is about the most natural way of eliciting one of the most wonderful gifts the Almighty has bequeathed us, the gift of laughter. In fact, it's so innate that, for the overwhelming majority of us, my better half included, it is an inherent and undeniable element of our physical composition. Touch certain areas of the skin and our sensory receptors spring to life, sending messages to the brain: "We're being tickled, it feels funny." How could anybody object to that?

But I imagine it's what comes next that separates some people—how the brain interprets the sensory messages received. It would appear that the interpretation can be either, *Relax, this feels funny, but it's natural* or, *Tense up, this is wrong.* And if wrong is the brain's response, it no longer feels good, it can't feel good.

Obviously, some tickling is inappropriate. Whether it's the participant, situation, intention, or any combination of these, inappropriate tickling will illicit undesirable feelings and unpredictable reactions. Once a questionable situation is experienced, each subsequent instance, regardless of intentions, becomes guilty by association. These situations can evolve into long-term psychological issues, and are most definitely beyond the scope of this passage.

Everyone else relax, it's only tickling.

What's the origin of this issue anyway? My guess is that, the most prevalent roots can be traced back to matters of trust and control. Think about it, to really experience pleasure when tickled, one has to be willing to relinquish control, to be guided by nothing but the sheer physical pleasure felt. (The young are much better equipped for such uncontrolled and unadulterated enjoyment.) To be comfortable being tickled, one has to set aside trust and control issues, assigning a premium to the simple enjoyment of the here and now.

Thinking about this tradeoff, it occurred to me that being tickled is really a metaphor for a committed relationship. The only way to truly get the most out of either is to cast aside the need to control, trust the bond between you and your partner, and simply enjoy each and every sensation together.

I'm reminded of a motivational speaker that told the story of a woman in one of his sessions who was not happy in her marriage. Upon further probing, it was revealed that the core problem was one of trust. It seems a past marriage, in which she had completely trusted her spouse had ended in significant pain—with him proving not to be worthy of her trust. By her admission, there was no way she would ever let herself be hurt that way again. As a result, she didn't believe she could ever relinquish the need to control or fully trust anyone again.

The motivational speaker asked her if she'd ever driven a car. A little perplexed, she responded that she had. The speaker then asked if, while driving a car, she had ever had the occasion to find herself driving down a two lane road, one lane headed in each direction. Not sure where his line of questioning was leading, she answered she had.

He then questioned whether she had any control over the traffic in the oncoming lane. She replied that, obviously, she did not. Bringing his questioning to a close, he wondered if she had no control over drivers in the oncoming vehicles and if someone who wasn't as committed to safety as she was could cause her serious harm, why had she ever driven on a road like that. "I just had to take that risk to get where I wanted to go," she answered.

"Oh," responded the motivational speaker.

If you happen to be one of the guarded ones, change. Find a way to trust and let go sometimes. It's the only way to stop missing out on the best that life has to offer.

And if you happen to be shopping around for Mr. or Ms. Right, you might try gauging the response of any prospective to the tickle test. It may just provide a little insight into any trust and control-related tendencies, and potentially even capacity for openness in the relationship.

As for me, I've already found my Ms. Right. However since I've seen evidence of some of these tendencies in our relationship as a whole—I guess Ms. Right and I have got a little talking to do.

> To ultimately realize a lifetime of love, love must be passionately molded, openly offered, and unconditionally received, one day at a time.

Wipe the Tears from Her Eyes

Wipe the tears from her eyes
Make all the hurt go away
Tell her that in tomorrow
There is hope in a new day

Shield her from the danger
Keep the bad people at bay
Tell her about the positive
Let nothing interrupt her play

Watch what she sees on TV
Tell her what's right to say
Teach her to do the right thing
All the love in my heart convey

Spend lots of time with her
A role model she can portray
And with all that I'm nervous
She starts kindergarten today

> Family is the ultimate natural resource; harvest it and reap its redeeming fortune.

The Purpose of Snow

A movie I rented, *Thirteen Conversations About One Thing*, some time back depicted the stories of a number of seemingly unconnected people whose lives through circumstance and fate, seemingly randomly intersect, the most telling of which was the chance meeting later in the movie between an older man and a young woman.

Regardless of the circumstances, the older gentleman had a reputation of always being in a positive mood. From his perspective, his twenty-three–year-long marriage was good. His job as an insurance claims examiner was good. Pretty much everything about his life, especially his attitude, was always good. His upbeat attitude was such a constant that his coworkers had given him the nickname Smiley. As time went on, Smiley's good-natured eternal art for finding a positive spin was enough to drive his cynical, divorced, and alone manager raving mad.

Partially to earn a coveted promotion and partially to teach a lesson, the manager boasted to a coworker he could surely remove that too familiar smile from Smiley's face. Smiley was told, because of financial problems at the company, he was being let go. Adjusting to the shock, Smiley offered condolences for the manager's difficult role. Then thinking out loud that he should look at it from the bright side, he continued, perhaps this would give him the opportunity to finally take a vacation, and spend some quality time with his children. True to form, Smiley left the office for the last time with a wave and his signature smile.

Separately, a young idealistic woman, convinced that everything in life has purpose, contently cleaned the apartments of the wealthy while daydreaming about the affections of her favorite client. One evening, while returning the voluntarily-mended shirt of her most admired customer, she was the victim of a hit and run. Found bleeding and unconscious, her recuperation proved both difficult and extensive. Managing to overcome considerable physical and psychological hurdles, eventually, she felt whole enough to again see the object of her long standing, secret, all-consuming affection.

With mended shirt in hand, she excitedly yet pensively waited for him to open his door. Following a couple questions about her medical condition, he proceeded to ask if she could return the watch he believed stolen. Devastated he could ever think that of her, she removed it from the drawer where she'd placed it for safe keeping, then abruptly exited his apartment for the final time.

Convinced that everything she ever believed in and everything she ever cared about was for naught, she found herself at a busy intersection contemplating suicide. Before stepping out into the oncoming traffic, she decided she would look for one last sign. She selected a stranger across the crowded intersection as a final indicator. In the absence of some sign, some telling action from that unwitting pedestrian, her life she was prepared to end. As she watched and readied herself to step off the curb, the stranger looked up, caught her eye, and smiled at her. Luckily, fate, in the guise of the termination slip just received, had placed Smiley on the opposite street corner in the middle of that day.

Maybe you're thinking, interesting premise for a movie; but real life doesn't work that way. What if our lives are, in fact, actually intertwined that way? I'm reminded of a past discussion I had with a retiring security guard.

After countless years of gainful employment, the soon to be eighty-six-year–old, Mr. Snow, had accepted that it was finally time to move on. Having seen the degree of pride he'd exhibited on a daily basis, I inquired whether he thought he would sincerely miss the job. He responded that, because of his plans, he didn't believe so, figuring that writing his autobiography would keep him sufficiently occupied.

Amazed by this surprising revelation, I was curious about the lessons learned over the course of his life. I questioned what he expected to be the core message of his story. I questioned what the most meaningful lesson was that he desired to pass on. He responded that, in this life, he has learned to attempt to offer a kind word to most everyone he interacts with. This, he explained, is important because we never know the effect a kind word or gesture will have on the recipient. He suggested I consider the possibility that any one of my fellow coworkers arriving that morning could be burdened with incredibly overwhelming problems, that for any one of them, suicide could be being considered as the only way out. He continued that we never know when a kind word might be one thing that could save the day. (Sound familiar?)

I left the discussion feeling energized and blessed to have been the beneficiary of such a powerful, inspiring construct that morning, at a time I was least expecting. I headed to my desk with an even greater respect for the apparent wealth of experiences, fortitude, and amassed perspective housed in such a quiet, unassuming frame. The brief conversation had fostered a bounce in my step and a newfound personal perspective on the relevance of my attitude in the lives of others.

In this life it's not likely we will ever fully comprehend the extent of our purpose or the impact we can, will, and already have had. It's not likely we will ever fully comprehend or appreciate how interwoven our lives have been with countless family members, friends, acquaintances, and strangers or the potential future magnitude of our relevance in so many encounters to come. It's not likely we will ever fully grasp why things happen the way they do. In this life, we simply will likely never know.

Therefore, maintaining a positive attitude, consistently striving to be at our best and perceiving every encounter as an opportunity to make a difference ensures the optimum readiness, come what may. From there, chance and circumstance can be counted on to handle the rest.

Putting this perspective in action one day, I can remember a coworker's fascination with me that I would invest the time to bid a great day to someone who mistakenly called my cell phone. Our conversation afterward reminded me of a college incident that was, until then, tucked away in the seldom-breached recesses of my mind.

As crank calls were not exactly unusual phenomena for my college dormitory, creative approaches were routinely devised for handling them. Simply hanging up was neither particularly interesting nor effective enough. And anyway, where was the fun in that? A common objective was to attempt to frustrate the crank caller into hanging up.

So there I was, with one such caller ringing my phone late one Saturday night, except this crank call was anything but ordinary. For starters, this caller was female. Just the same, there was the customary exchange of familiar crank-call pleasantries with her attempting to embarrass me, and me continuously raising the stakes. That is until I asked the question that would transition the conversation to a level all its own.

I asked how was it that a young woman such as herself had nothing better to do on a Saturday night than make crank phone calls. I asked, "Shouldn't you be somewhere instead having a good time with your friends?" Well, my questions opened the floodgates, as, over the next hour or so, her answers were revealed. As far as true friends were concerned, she had none. She wasn't hopeful or happy with her current prospects, her looks, or her life. And she didn't foresee much opportunity for improvement. She finally confessed she had begun to seriously contemplate suicide as the only viable way out of her misery.

Although I initially pondered the possibility her story could be false, the apparent sincerity of her words and tone, and the time invested, served to assure me differently. These considerations, along with a quick moment's consideration as to the potential gravity of the situation, were enough to sufficiently eliminate questions on my part.

Into the wee hours of the next morning, I tried to convince the unidentified voice at the opposite end of the conversation that things inevitably would not turn out as barren and hopeless as she feared. I suggested alternative paths and perspectives, asked about her aspirations and dreams, and tried to convince her that her life was precious, far too precious to, at any juncture, even consider cutting it short.

Given the duration of the call and the extent of topics discussed, my sense and hope was that the discussion was having a meaningful effect on her. That is until mid-sentence, when the call was abruptly lost. I waited anxiously, seemingly trying to will my phone to ring again. (These were the days before ubiquitous caller ID and *69, so if getting back to her was an option, it was an option that I didn't know. My suspicion was that she was in a similar predicament, since I was likely just a randomly dialed call.)

That was it. The opportunity to influence had come and gone. Our individual realities would continue to traverse their different paths, not likely destined to intersect again, and perhaps permanently altered even if not completely understood. Nevertheless, time and (I hoped) both of our lives would carry on.

Initially, some perplexing questions lingered concerning that fateful night and the surrounding circumstances. What would prompt someone contemplating seriously the notion of suicide to spend time making a crank phone call? Why did the conditions happen to be just right, me at home that night, with nothing else going on, with no roommate or friends around – permitting my undivided attention to be focused on the call? What was it that caused my friends and me, shortly beforehand, to begin making a contest of actively engaging crank callers? In today's full-disclosure age of caller ID, would this type of perceived veiled "cry for help" even be possible? Out of all the possibilities, how was it my number she dialed?

I've come to believe that these events were simply necessary for the fulfillment of a greater purpose. And given the uncertainty of the outcome, I can only hope, when it counted the most that my best got the job done—much the way Smiley's did.

While some may question the legitimacy, of the young lady's confession, for me, little doubt lingers. Given the stakes and the fact that I don't know of a way to definitely gauge the honesty of a soul bared, accepting her plausible story was an option viable enough for me. After all, when it's all said and done, we should aspire to engage each situation encountered in this life positively. In that way, the vast potential of our capacity for meaningful impact can have no limit other than that which is fostered by our very best.

My sense is, Smiley must have understood this. While his role was not a leading one in the movie, because of the magnitude of his influence, he was undoubtedly one of the most significant forces. My sense is the gentleman who retired, understands this and, even at his age, the extent of his potential impact in the lives of others has no bounds. Perhaps we will all have the opportunity to be positively influenced by his published words one day.

Who knows? Maybe one of the since born offspring of my, young, distraught caller will, one day, refer to this very passage in an effort to inspire someone in need. Just think about it: his or her very existence alone would offer stark evidence of the affect that one event, that one interaction, can have on numerous lives. Further, any meaningful impact that resulted would bare witness to just how intimately connected our otherwise seemingly individual existences truly are, how interconnected your and my existences are truly meant to be.

Endeavor to meet each purpose head-on, to positively influence every situation that arises, and to face each new encounter with a smile—these are all worthwhile objectives to which we should aspire. For much the same way the appearance of a few falling snowflakes can so readily resurrect the wonder and enthusiasm of even the most tainted youth, each of us inherently possesses the power within to quietly and effectively change the world.

Amazingly, all it takes to get started is a little consideration and a smile.

Just prior to his last day of work, I stopped by to visit the soon-to-be retiree. Bearing a gift, an instructional reference guide for would-be new authors, I thanked him for his attitude and positive impact. I asked whether he had any indication of the degree of influence he'd had over the years. He answered that the most telling indication for him had occurred some time back when a young woman confessed that she had, on a given day, decided she was going to take her life. She told him, merely hours away from the planned event, his positive outlook and words that fateful day had made a difference.

Even more inspired by the power of his quiet and unassuming presence, I asked whether he felt, given his age and health, he would have the stamina to accomplish his mission to share the message of his life with the world. He looked at me, let out a broad smile and said, "God willing."

Because Mr. Snow's message is just the type we need a little more of in this world, I hope for his, your, and my sakes, God *is* willing.

Through You

Rarely do we get such a majestic sign
Something so naturally pure and true
The result of inspired commitment
And effort that nurtures a lasting value

As evidenced by the people impacted
And enlightenment that comes through
It's apparent that in his glorious way
The Lord touches us all through you

Jessica, Not Quite So Normal

When flipping through TV stations, it's not uncommon to come across stories of hardship, misfortune, and disability. When faced with these stories, many of us hasten to turn away. Not only does avoidance serve to maintain our more upbeat mode, it effectively minimizes any feelings of depression or guilt, any increased feelings of obligation to make a greater impact in the time we have.

Every once in a while, however, before there is an opportunity to ignore, something manages to slip through our carefully constructed cocoon of self-absorption. And once our self-inflicted state of interpersonal ignorance is interrupted, and we are forced to consider someone else's predicament, we can't help but do that which we so diligently tried to avoid. We begin to care. Such is the case in Jessica's story.

Jessica was a beautiful baby, born to a loving mother and father. Yet while it didn't lessen one iota of the love her family felt for her, Jessica was born with no arms.

Okay, quite honestly, this would typically be the point where I would begin to reach for the remote. Not because I am uncaring, mind you, more aptly just the opposite. In the past, as it relates to unwarranted human affliction, I've taken myself through the gamut. My feelings have ranged from guilt (for not always appreciating how blessed I am) to irritation (toward so many others who are not cognitive of, and so ultimately waste, the many talents and endowments with which they have been blessed), to temporary disillusionment with faith. After all, how can a just God allow so many unfortunate events to afflict so many undeserving people while so many of the ill-intentioned remain unaffected? How can so much drive and desire be permitted to perish, uselessly, in many doomed to exist without the capabilities and means to exploit it while others with all the tools and opportunities in the world simply waste it? It's easier to change the channel. However, Jessica didn't give me that chance.

The first thing I noticed was her absolutely amazing attitude. Simply put, Jessica was a confident, outspoken, intelligent, energetic, enthusiastic, fun-loving teenager. She earned excellent grades, had a happy and loving family, had plenty of friends, and, oh yeah, happened to have no arms.

Intermixed with the young woman's upbeat and hopeful perspective was commentary from family and friends, along with remarkable video of how she has managed to conquer any and all odds placed in her path. Her father discussed her incredible will even as a baby, readily adapting and seemingly never discouraged. Jessica, focusing on what she did have, taught herself to become as proficient with her legs, feet, and toes as many are with their arms, hands, and fingers.

Jessica can take care of herself, adeptly dressing and preparing food for herself and her family. She has mastered countless skills, which we usually take for granted, including writing, counting money, and using a PC. She's also mastered other skills that aren't generally common at all, such as a few years earlier when she decided she wanted to drive a tractor. At the time of the taping, Jessica's latest passion was becoming a dynamite cheerleader. And no surprise, head-on is the way she was vigorously, enthusiastically, and fearlessly attacking this latest objective, just the way she does everything else she encounters.

I sat there, astonished and completely captivated, with a smile on my face and a spirit unexpectedly enlightened by the immenseness of the will and presence possessed by the amazing young woman. Jessica, however, maintains a different outlook. Through her eyes, none of these accomplishments represent notable feats. Jessica would rather be perceived as a normal person, living a normal life. Her belief is that she's not special. She has merely utilized the capabilities God has blessed her with. In this casual observer's opinion, if she doesn't want to be considered special, she will need to lose that attitude. Because, the reality is, it is her attitude that makes her so utterly remarkable.

In the comedy *Bruce Almighty*, the protagonist asks God what he would have him do. God, in the guise of Morgan Freeman, responds, "See, that's the problem, everyone is always looking up for answers." Jessica seems to have come to this realization early in life. Instead of looking up and asking why, she most certainly must face the mirror and question why not.

As the human-interest cable offering was drawing to a close, Jessica was asked whether she ever questioned why she was put here as she was. Thoughtfully, she responded that she believes she was put on earth to serve as an inspiration to others. She continued that it was her hope that, through her, regardless of their circumstances, others would know they can achieve whatever they put their minds to.

As far as maintaining her perspective, Jessica indicated she has learned to be who she is regardless of the fact that she was not born "normal." One thing became blatantly obvious while watching her story: she is correct, she is truly anything but "normal."

My contention is that we all could benefit from learning something from Jessica's example. Perhaps we should all be striving to be a little less normal, and a little more like her. Perhaps we would all benefit from a little more commitment and passionate pursuit of our aspirations, a few less excuses, and an additional mirror or two.

After seeing Jessica's story, I'm more committed than ever to the aggressive pursuit of my dreams. After all, even my most logical excuses, in comparison, have been essentially rendered immaterial. What about you? Do any of your excuses hold up?

Thanks Jessica. Your engaging spirit inspires opportunity where others might find only limitations, unlimited promise where others would be inclined to despair. You've proven that a smile and a healthy dose of determination trumps all, in the process, giving us the most worthy of inspirational targets for which to shoot.

I wish you the best of luck in your anything-but-normal life.

> When you give unconditionally from the heart, the love touches all.

Sometimes

Sometimes in life you search
Many times without even a clue
Whether you will find someone special
The one person in this world for you

In relationships you find yourself
Longing for a love that's really true
Always giving the best you have
Always finding more adjustments due

Sometimes...

But sometimes you find him or her
Whether a familiar face or out of the blue
Like an incredible ray of sunlight
Souls connect; one heart is born from two

And suddenly things are different
Every raindrop, every sunrise is so new
You experience the joy of life together
After each discussion you find you grew

Sometimes...

And sometimes you try to figure it out
Exactly what changed, what did you do
Just love and be loved on this day
And be thankful this sometime is for you

Sometimes...

Mission 4

Browse your phonebook and locate someone special whom you haven't spoken to in a while. Pick up the phone and give them a call within the next day or two. Relive some old times, and take the time to inform them how much they mean to you. Then, after letting them know what prompted your long overdue call, challenge them to take the time to contact someone special in return. And if you enjoyed it, open your phonebook again.

A Little Gratitude

True happiness and fulfillment begin by acknowledging and appreciating what we are blessed to have. By emphasizing what's positive around us, by taking time to notice and enjoy the little things, by realizing there are others that never had, and by not losing sight that things could be worse, we will never forget that, via our perspective, attitude and actions, we always have the power to improve things. So, a little gratitude...

Being Blessed

After a long day, I exited my place of employment, once again having over-stayed my intended time of departure. Outside, in the seasonally warm evening air, I paused momentarily to look, to listen, and I was truly amazed. What I saw were vibrant colors all across the sky—purple, orange, red, blue, streaks of white, beautiful clouds, and the magnificent golden glow of the setting sun just over the horizon. Birds, oblivious to the ills of man's world gracefully, seemingly happily, glided by. Individual trees, not yet presenting their full complement of leaves, cut incredible silhouettes against the artistry of the evening sky. I simply stood there, in awe.

The same trees, unnoticed during my hurried trip that morning, and most other days, now possessed a whole new relativity, a whole new meaning. I heard the angelic sounds of birds with beautifully perfected songs all around me—songs no different from proceeding days and nights, except this particular night, I listened.

But because I interrupted the hustle and bustle of my life, because I took the time to notice, that day, without a doubt, I knew that I was blessed. I was blessed for the enlightenment and perspective instilled that day, blessed for all that goes unheard, unseen, unnoticed, unappreciated, and un-thanked each and every day, simply blessed.

Thus, on behalf of every one of us, I humbly say, "Thank you, Lord."

Morning

From my unknowing slumber, I awake to find a new day
And for the split second it takes to accumulate my wits,
I subconsciously pause to ponder, to reflect
On yesterday, today, tomorrow, on myself

Shall I focus on
The sorrow that found me and ruined my yesterday
Or the fact that I got through it, challenged yet okay

Shall I focus on
The aches that more and more often come my way
Or the wisdom of years that grows stronger everyday

Shall I focus on
Relationships lost, missed loved ones taken away
Or friends and family here now loving me each day

Shall I focus on
The lost manners, the lack of courtesy people display
Or the smiles derived from the thank you's that I say

Shall I focus on
The stress, the difficulties that seem to come my way
Or the amazing power I possess to make an impact today

A second later a familiar realization lights the way
Yesterday is no longer mine to contemplate
And tomorrow never was
All I really have is today and myself

I stretch, smile, decide to open my eyes
I will not waste another second of this gift, my new day

A Full Swing

Have you ever felt that things simply don't tend to work out for you? Do you sometimes feel that a good percentage of your efforts are fruitless and never even approach success? Well, not to worry. Here's an interesting little story heard along the way, which might serve to provide some perspective.

A man visits his priest and reports that he feels like a complete failure. "I don't know what it is, but it seems I fail at half of the things I do," he complains. The priest asks him to go read a particular page in the World Book Almanac and return the next day. The man returns the next day, visibly upset.

"I came here at the end of my rope, looking for help and you offered me nothing."

"Didn't you locate the information to which I directed you?"

"Sure, but a lifetime batting average of three hundred-something has nothing to do with me or my feelings of depression!"

"Sure it does," responded the priest. "You see, it's simple, here's a professional player celebrated for holding the world record even though he failed two out of three times he got up to bat. If you are batting .500, all I can say to you is, keep up the great work!"

Fortunately, life isn't intended to be comprised of an endless string of homeruns. Fortunately, because can you imagine how monotonous and boring that would be? No, in this life what really qualifies us to appreciate, enjoy, get the most out of, and to be truly worthy of the good times is having effectively survived, learned, and grown from the bad ones. In other words, it is intimate knowledge of the lowest lows that makes the highest high seem awesome.

Life doesn't end if you don't, this time, hit a homerun. However, life doesn't truly begin until you are willing to step up to the plate. So go ahead and step up. Have the confidence that you will get the most out of the experience. Have the confidence that you will do your best. When a pitch looks good, take a full swing, and give it everything you're worth. Be ready and willing to respond to whatever comes next. And always remember to be positive, smile often, and have a little fun with it—after all, it's supposed to be a game.

Batter up!

Thankfully, when we are least expecting it, the most incredible possibilities can reveal themselves. As a result, it's paramount we keep our eyes peeled, our spirits lifted, and our perspectives open. For it's only when we are duly prepared, that life's incredible potential is capable of happening for us.

Into Each Life, Some Rain Must Fall

After a long day at the office, waiting in heavy rush-hour traffic adversely impacted by pretty constant rain, I had the distinct pleasure to find myself in an interesting discussion with two children. We stood in the rain, each under a separate umbrella.

Asked if they'd had good days, both confirmed they had. I then requested they share with me what made the day such a good one. One indicated it was getting to work on a school project. The other responded having her test returned was the highlight. When I asked if they could guess the best part of my day, after a few guesses, they confessed to having no further ideas. I then repositioned my umbrella so it was down at my side.

Standing there in my suit, I allowed the rain to fall unobstructed onto my face. I stood there for a few seconds, feeling the coldness of the rain, of each individual raindrop finding my face, then running off on its own distinctive track. At that point, not much else mattered—not the day, what needed to be done after, not much else. I turned to the girls, smiled, and declared, "This is the best part of my day." (I don't stop to do things like that enough during the course of my days. I need to work on that. I need to make the time to do them more often.)

As we were wrapping up the conversation, I offered one parting comment for the two young ladies to consider. I told them the reason this particular act was so meaningful to me was my belief that when we are touched by a fallen raindrop, that's about as close as we can get, in this lifetime, to being actually touched by heaven.

With that, the girls then followed suit, each taking their umbrellas from above their heads. Together we stood, joyfully experiencing the cascading rain, treasuring each passing moment, appreciating heaven's touch.

Just a little something to think about the next time a bit of rain enters your life, the next time you're concerned about getting a little wet.

Momma, I Love You

Momma, I love you

For the ups, the downs,
The unconditional love over the years,
For all the worrying,
Often called meddling, for the quiet tears

Momma,

For the pain of delivery,
Rejoicing because limbs were in pairs
For giving of yourself,
Constantly demonstrating a mother cares

Momma,

You have sacrificed your life;
You're there whenever trouble nears
Your faith makes me stronger;
Your encouragement quells my fears

Momma,

Through it all you ask for nothing,
No awards, no heroic cheers
You watch over me in silence,
You vouch for me in your prayers

Momma,

Now that I am older,
I sometimes can get caught up in my affairs
I have even taken you for granted;
My need to be me often interferes

Momma,

But wherever I go and whatever I do,
No matter what the future bears
I will always admire, respect, and
Love you; know that no one compares

Momma

In Time

When was the last time you felt powerless? Have you ever really felt lost, ignored, victimized, or forgotten? When was the last time you felt completely alone? Imagine how overwhelming it would be to feel that way on a regular basis. Imagine the despair. Imagine the helplessness. It's difficult to comprehend, huh? Well, chances are we won't have difficulty comprehending this... in time.

Part of a previous job within the financial industry entailed, on a monthly basis, interfacing by phone with our customers. In addition to responding to account queries and executing account adjustments, I tried to positively affect the customer's mood and situation whenever possible. During one particular call, I wasn't able to effectively enhance anything. To the contrary, this call left me in a self-imposed state of despair. The gentleman, senior in years, explained with difficulty his tenuous predicament. After growing progressively worse the last few years, his eyesight had finally deteriorated to a legally-blind status. He had neither family nor any other dependable assistance, with the exception of his aging wife with her own significantly diminished health and capabilities. For years, squinting and utilization of magnifying glasses had been the means by which he managed their affairs. Now these mechanisms were no longer viable.

As I listened to this humble yet obviously proud man with his lifetime of experiences, I painstakingly attempted to imagine what he must have been feeling. I considered how difficult it must have been to work so hard and long to manage the affairs for his family, home, himself, only to see his control dwindling with each passing day.

In no way was the gentleman complaining, however. He wasn't looking for sympathy. And he certainly wasn't seeking a hand out. The gentleman was merely informing me, in a proud yet apologetic tone, that his fixed income and other bills would not allow a payment of $500 for the month. He confessed he had no idea how previous months' statements had been overlooked; however unfortunately he could only afford his standard monthly payment of $150 dollars.

As I listened to his story, I felt for the gentleman. He had absolutely no one to look out for him. He had no one to help manage his affairs, no one to help him understand. My guess was that during the time when the gentleman grew up, a loan was money you got from someone who cared about you and your predicament. You borrowed the money, said thanks, and paid it back as soon as you could. The gentleman probably didn't even begin to comprehend what it meant to borrow small sums of money over time and watch your balance creep continuously upward, along with escalating fees and annual percentage rates. Somewhere, in the back of his mind, he was probably trying to figure out how he could pay money back each month and never really see the amount owed decrease. He had no one to explain to him that on a ten-thousand-dollar loan, with a 20 percent interest rate, 80 percent of his minimum monthly payment doesn't go toward paying off the loan. And to make it worse, he had other loans with other institutions.

When the call ended, I just sat there thinking about his predicament. How did he get to this place? Shouldn't there have been some kind of protection against this sort of thing? Where was the fairness, the allowances that were supposed to come from a lifetime of doing the best you could? Where were his family and friends? Where were the people who could help him understand?

Each day the people our society should treasure and protect most, the people from whom we have the most to learn, find themselves in this situation. Organizations that neither know nor particularly care about their situations are more than willing to extend long-term, high-interest loans. Seniors, whether because there is nowhere else to turn, because of pride and the desire to remain self-reliant, or because they do not understand the ramifications, willingly accept these loans. And whether it's to pay for rent, that all-important gift for a grandchild, a "loan" for a struggling family member, that perfect appliance especially target-marketed to them on a TV shopping channel, mail and phone scams, food for the week, or the ever more expensive medicine required to make the pain go away, the bills mount, the financial hole deepens. Imagine what it must feel like to be between their rock and hard place.

Don't our parents, grandparents, uncles, aunts, and neighbors deserve better in the later years of their life. After a lifetime of dedication, effort, perseverance, concern, hopes, and dreams, don't the senior members of our society deserve a little more than being ignored, forgotten about, taken advantage of, and, even worse, abused. Throughout history, most civilizations have held their elders in the highest esteem and treated their wisdom with the greatest of respect. Why don't we? If we don't begin to do something about their cycle of pain, what will that say about our society? What will that say about us? And what will we be teaching our youth? If we don't address this cycle of pain, what will we have to look forward to? Will advanced years bring us similar confusion, alienation, lack of control, and despair? Will we grow to know what it feels like to be forgotten about, to feel unappreciated?

Only our actions and time will tell.

Thank You

Thank you, Mom,
For having me, sheltering me,
Teaching and loving me so

Thank you, Dad,
For protecting me, the morals
And for the inspiration to grow

Thank you, siblings,
For years of caring, sharing,
The many highs and occasional low

Thank you, teachers,
For your time, commitment,
The foundation of things I know

Thank you, church,
For the moral fiber and faith,
The origins of my spiritual glow

Thank you, friends,
For the laughs, conversations,
And support that you show

Thank you, all,
For a lifetime of memories,
Every kind gesture, every hello

Thank you, Lord,
For the blessings, and for
My future home, held in escrow

Thank you.

The More Things Change

I was sitting there, looking out the window on what had become a quiet, hot Saturday afternoon. The rain was falling, the trees swaying, the thunder roaring, and an occasional streak of lighting made its way across an otherwise somewhat dreary sky. As my momma used to tell us, this was the Lord's time.

And it wasn't the best timing either. I had plans for the day. I had been determined to spend the bulk of the day working on SomethingToShare.com related initiatives. The objective was to maintain focus on my work and to have a productive day. Instead, a passing storm had forced me to turn off my PC and sit there watching and waiting, just like when I was growing up.

My mom didn't play when it came to thunderstorms. Anything and everything electrical had to be shut off and unplugged. No phone calls, no running around, "get away from that window," no playing (although sometimes we did get away with doing so quietly), no music, nothing. Typically, my siblings and I were assembled in the living room together with my mom to wait it out.

I can remember it all being an issue for me. The storms always seemed to come at inappropriate times. The dreaded clasp of thunder would occur when I wanted to watch something special on television, when I wanted to be outside, when I had important things to do. I would be stuck in silence with my brother, sisters, and mother until who knew when. And what was the purpose anyway? Oh sure, we had heard the explanations over the years, ranging from us needing to show respect for the Lord's time to not wanting us to be struck, to a story my mom heard growing up about a child being struck and killed, to the ritual being what her mother used to do. None of these reasons hit the mark for at least one of us.

Don't get me wrong, I had respect for God. It was why I prayed and went to Sunday school. However, I had seen a good number of storms and I knew a lot of people who knew a lot of people and none of them had ever gotten struck by lightning, whether they were talking and playing or not. Furthermore, not one television, radio, or game within that radius that I knew of had been demolished by the weather. So why did we have to interrupt our plans and huddle around in virtual silence? I promised myself "one day."

I was off to college soon enough, on my own. Sure enough, during thunderstorms, I could watch television and do whatever else I wanted to. My logic held up without a hitch. My electronics and I remained catastrophe-free. I graduated and eventually bought a house for my mom to come and live with me. Invariably, the first thunderstorm came. But things were different now. I was an adult. So there I was while she turned off everything and sat quietly in another part of the house doing what I pleased.

My mom would pass away just a few months later.

It's funny the things you think about when you lose someone you love, funny the things you wish you could just take back. Now I would give anything I have to be able to sit through one more thunderstorm with my mom. And I couldn't care less about any of those shows on television, the music, or anything going on outside.

So there I sat with everything turned off, watching the Lord's work, respectful of the majesty of it all. I realized that that is what it was, and is, all about. It was about respecting the Lord. It was about slowing down. It was about being around the people that loved us. It was about tradition. It was about reminding us that there were things bigger than we. It was about caring. It was about simple times. It was about respecting Mom's wishes. It was about then and now. It was about a mother's love. It was about not moving so fast that we lose track of where we needed to be. It was about doing what we were told—whether we understood it or not. It was about time and how we spend it. It was about loving my mother and what she stood for. It was about the glory of God.

That day, I came to better understand that.

By the time the storm headed off in the distance, I had new direction. I had come to realize that no matter what I accomplished when I turned the PC back on, it would pale in comparison to the understanding and impact that brief thunderstorm had brought my way. I can now anticipate my family huddled quietly in one room during future storms, the kids silently cursing the storm and me. I can see it clearly now.

And I just know Mom is smiling.

> Above all, stay humble, motivated, and impressionable. Know that you are blessed, opportunities abound, and life isn't quite finished with you yet.

Taken for Granted

Unbeknownst to the others, with just a hint of a smile, a couple of slightly watery eyes, and an enlightened heart, I returned to my seat. In the few minutes that I had been out of the meeting, my perspective had been completely altered. I had gained a new appreciation for the very much familiar objective I had just accomplished, and what was truly important had taken on, at least for a little while, a whole new meaning.

I was in the middle of my third and final day of offsite meetings and very much focused on making the most of the remaining time our small team had to progress toward our objective. Finally, giving in to nature's persistent and, by then, persuasive call, I hustled off in search of the restroom, intent on quickly getting back to the effort at hand.

Managing to locate the restroom, I ducked in and made my way in the direction of the closest urinal. As I turned the corner, I was startled to find another gentleman already in the area with his wheelchair positioned diagonally in front of two of the three urinals. Not having the luxury to spend a lot of time contemplating the situation, I hurriedly maneuvered myself past the chair's handle and in front of the vacant urinal.

As I stood there, the sense of relief I was experiencing would take a backseat to an intensifying feeling of awkwardness about the situation. It had just occurred to me that one of the business areas housed in the facility employed a considerable number of adults with impairments. As I had initially maneuvered past the chair, my peripheral vision caught him fumbling to open a cup. Shortly after, while I could hear him apparently struggling, I couldn't readily tell whether he was actually experiencing a problem of some type. As I finished up, I found myself somewhat indecisive, not quite sure of exactly what to do. I definitely wasn't comfortable with the possibility of needing to provide him assistance; however, there was no possibility I would ignore him if he was truly in need. And I certainly did not want to embarrass him. I stood there knowing there was no reason for me to be embarrassed but a little embarrassed just the same.

Once finished, I maneuvered back past the chair and headed over to the sink. As he appeared to be no longer struggling, my mind began to wander as I washed my hands. How many times had I, over the course of my life, been able to do something as simple as walk to the bathroom and utilize the facilities with no effort, no discomfort, no specialized tools or devices, without the slightest degree of recognition or appreciation for how fortunate I am? How many times had I been able to stand up, sit down, lie down, walk, run, see something, hear something, smell something, feel something, eat something, drink something, think about something, remember something, create something, read something, understand something, without even the least possible degree of consideration or gratitude? How many times had I effortlessly been able to do all these things without the realization that countless people spend a lifetime either struggling to do them or never being able to do them at all? Maybe I should have been embarrassed after all.

I began thinking a little more about the gentleman. How difficult it must be to go through all of that each time he needs to relieve himself and, even worse, how much more difficult bowel movements must be. As I contemplated all of this, my mind raced, and my heart began to fill. Why did he, or anyone else for that matter, have to endure all of this? I thought how difficult his life must be.

The door opened and another adult with an impairment made his way over to wash his hands.

"How are you?"

"Good," I responded, "how are you today?"

"Good, you know, we have a holiday coming on Friday. I can't wait."

The gentleman in the wheelchair (still finishing up at the urinals) happily piped in, "I know, I can't wait either."

I asked, "Won't the two of you miss not being at work on Friday?"

They each laughed and agreed neither would have a problem with not having to come to work.

As I left the restroom, I laughed and wished them each a great day off!

I walked out and into a crowd of adults with impairments, obviously on break. They were talking, laughing, and generally having a great time. I felt the beginnings of smile as I realized they weren't feeling sorry for themselves, and they certainly wouldn't want me feeling sorry for them. More to the point, I suspected I should probably strive to be more like them, to more consistently emulate their degree of inner strength, to strive to eliminate any time I spend feeling sorry for my own perceived impairments and deficiencies. And, last but not least, I reasoned I would greatly benefit from endeavoring to ensure the priorities in my life more often resembled some of theirs.

As I made it back to the conference room for the remainder of the meeting, I found myself a little less pressed about what we would accomplish the rest of the day, a little more amazed by some of the people working just down the hall, and determined to be a little more thankful the next time I was blessed enough to be able to simply get up and go answer nature's call.

What a productive day it was.

Mission 5

Start a new habit. Find someone, preferably someone you do not know, who does not appear to be having a good day and pay them a compliment, tell them a joke. Whatever it takes, make it your objective to create a smile where none existed before. By example, remind them that whatever burdens they might have, the best way to lighten them is to change their perspective. And the most effective way to begin to change perspective is simply to smile.

Do this once and watch the difference you'll make in that person's day. Do this on a daily basis and watch the difference you'll make in yours.

Playing With Passion

Now is not the time for being timid, tentative, or content. Now is not the time for flying under the radar. If we want to be our best, live life to the fullest and make a difference, then now is the time to be audacious, to be dreamers and believe in ourselves. Now is the time and virtually anything is possible. This is the time to be neither fearful nor a spectator, because truly living is playing with passion.

Time Is

In the most relevant sense, time isn't about anything found on the face of a watch. No, in the truest sense, time is life. Time is redemption. Time is where we were, where we are, and where we are going. Time is the quality we derive of each day, once gone, gone forever. Time is perspective, one's ability to come to see things in a more constructive way. Time is growth, continuous, correcting the attitudes, beliefs, and behaviors in need of such. Time is meaning, and the search for that meaning in all things, big and small. Time is loved ones, not the quantity, but the quality, the value of relationships nurtured, knowing you've found someone who also believes in you. Time is coming to love who you are and who you will endeavor to one day be. Time is coming to appreciate all the majesty and the magnificent blessings that surround us each day. Time is ever-stronger faith in the Almighty, in you, in a better tomorrow. Time is a single, solitary thought, and the difference that, one day, it could bring. Time is the potential to change a dream into reality. Time is the tireless search for true happiness and fulfillment. Time is the never-ending search for greater love. Ultimately, it is time that will color the sketch that is our destiny. Time is, in every sense, our lives.

Waste it at your own peril.

> Genuine pride simply doesn't leave room for excuses.

Get In the Game

Why is it that some people virtually always seem to ride a wave of achievements and others do not? Why is it that, some continuously migrate ever closer to fulfillment of their dreams and others do not? Why is it that some regularly find and experience true and meaningful happiness in their lives and countless others do not? Is the latter group the equivalent of God's neglected stepchildren, undeserving of the opportunities that, for select others, are as natural as the light of day? Not likely.

Are the unfulfilled merely random martyrs, eternally condemned, never to understand or appreciate the extent to which they can, and do, control their destinies? Is their fate simply to mark the passage of time in an uninspired existence, forever mired in the status quo? That depends.

- ### The Formula Revealed

Suppose a surprisingly simple winning formula for life actually exists. Suppose, much like a well-designed, practiced, and executed game-plan in your sport of choice, one's life can be successfully scripted. And finally, suppose that once a game-plan has been initiated, success invariably comes down to the quality and consistency of choices made each day and the degree of the positive attitude incorporated to sustain them.

It could convincingly be argued that our present disposition in life has been most predominately defined by our choices in the past and tomorrow's potential by our choices today. In other words, the most crucial difference between those who possess success, prosperity, and happiness and those who do not is the collective tenor of the choices made, and whether an inspired attitude was, and continues to be, maintained to properly nurture those choices. As a result, the degree of individual success or failure we are destined to achieve, and the extent to which we will be intimately familiar with true and lasting happiness, is essentially up to each of us.

This perspective suggests our ongoing results are derivative of how we respond to those events and happenstances. It is the adoption and unconditional commitment to this mindset, and associated behaviors that most uniquely distinguish the truly happy from the unhappy, the successful from unsuccessful, the passionate from the discontented, the leaders from the followers. When it's all said and done, each of our lives truly is what we make of it.

To reap the greatest rewards, the nature, tenor, and perceived criticality of day-to-day decisions and associated behaviors must continuously be enhanced. In addition, ever-more-challenging and wider-reaching perspectives must be embraced, perspectives that both govern and elevate not only our decisions and attitudes but the very course of our lives. Armed with this mindset, it becomes increasingly impossible not to believe passionately in the power of your destiny. It becomes increasingly impossible not to invest unwavering belief in, and commitment to, your dreams and aspirations. It becomes impossible to believe that you can't change the world.

With this psyche duly engaged, time, especially that which remains will develop much greater significance. Nurtured by passion, purpose will find more and more fertile ground and grow. Once the roots of purpose begin to grow and the need for fulfillment finally takes hold, a future not founded on purpose, a future not utilizing the precious time we have remaining to the fullest, will cease to be, on any level, acceptable. Then life can really begin.

Just imagine the limitless potential of our greatest qualities enriched with a never-ending injection of passion. Imagine the potential force of those qualities, those talents, unchecked by fear of failure. Imagine an ever-expanding confidence in your abilities, fortified and empowered by a healthy supply of internal praise and anticipation for each and every looming triumph to come. Imagine having some place you need to be, some place your heart, your mind, and your spirit enthusiastically agree that it's where you ought to, no, *have* to be. Then, without concern for distance, undaunted by would-be-limiting doubt, you take a deep breath and step.

If you are true to adopting this mindset, taking that first step will be immensely gratifying. And it's that empowering feeling that will inspire each new incremental step to come. Each successive individual victory will mandate an ever-more committed you. Commit to this mindset and greater purpose and personal fulfillment will be fostered. Commit to this mindset, and your true intended destiny can be your own.

It comes down to perspective and choice. Will we crave personal growth and fulfillment enough to commit to this simple yet empowering life-enriching perspective? Will we endeavor to continuously enhance our perspective, to foster the best choices? Will we stand and represent, or will we cower and defer? In the end, it all starts and ends with the fundamental question: In the arena of life, will the essence of our true destiny be merely that of a spectator or will we be stars in the game?

Only time and our next steps will tell.

> Apathy is a state of mind, a desolate, stagnant, barren, psychologically debilitating state with an exorbitant cost of living. Don't even visit.

An Inside Job

How would you react if you realized that your most valuable possessions, over time, were being discretely stolen? First, to prevent future offenses, chances are an aggressive investigation would be undertaken to uncover who, what, how, and when. Then, with protection against future occurrences effectively deployed, it would be just a matter of time before restitution is sought. But what if the investigation reveals an inside job? It most certainly would add insult to injury to realize the culprit was someone you trusted.

What if the invaluable possessions lost weren't actually tangible? What if they were often underappreciated, life-affirming objectives, such as commitment to your hopes and dreams, true fulfillment in life, passion for living, the motivation to make a difference, and an unconditional belief in yourself and potential? Considering the value of these qualities to establishing the course of our lives, should our response be any less determined?

What would you do if your investigation revealed the perpetrator was really the closest insider of all—you? What would you do?

As inconceivable as that sounds, in reality, to some extent, this turns out to be pretty typical. On a daily basis, many of us unwittingly subject ourselves to an invasive, limiting thought process. Unchecked, these counterproductive thoughts can eventually become the catalyst for a lifelong assumption of contradicting roles, that of culprit and victim. How can that be? Well, actually it's fairly natural.

- ### The Limitation Spiral At Work

The *limitation spiral,* innocently enough, commences with the tacit acceptance of an unfounded personal limitation. Whether the result of an individual failed attempt or the precursor for effort never even applied, internal misgivings are allowed to germinate. Often, further nurtured by like-minded, even less motivated friends and acquaintances, the perceived limitation finds fertile ground for deep roots to grow. The limiting perspective results in lowered expectations and detrimental behavior. The detrimental behavior, in turn, yields ever more limited results, providing an even stronger foundation for additional doubt and blame. And so the spiral begins anew.

Given the self-perpetual nature of these spirals, as well as the typically ample supply of discouraging opinions readily found to further bolster any negative voices within, it's understandable that these limiting perceptions become embedded, embraced even, in the mindset of the oblivious victim over time.

It is important to note, however, that the mere presence of spirals in our lives does not necessarily denote lowered expectations and lack of achievement to come. Quite the contrary, amazingly self-sustaining, there are empowering behavior-enhancing spirals that can be tapped into to sustain, inspire, and elevate us to unprecedented drive and never-before-experienced heights. These motivating spirals, sometimes mistakenly written off as simple luck by the casual observer, integrate positive attitude, enhanced expectation, knowledge of previous efforts, and lots of diligence to script a significantly more encouraging perspective and, more often than not, considerably more achieving and rewarding outcomes.

The monumental influence of these spirals on both the nature of our aspirations and the magnitude of accomplishments to come suggests the criticality of the pivotal decision that each of us has made, and will make, countless times during the course of our lives. Whether we consciously realize it or not, by the nature of our response to each circumstance encountered, we determine if the spiral adopted will be positive or negative, and whether our result will more likely be enriching or limiting.

Perhaps the most vital distinction between habitual positive "spiralers" and their more numerous negative counterparts is the understanding that happiness is primarily a perceived derivative of our choices and perspective, both of which are within our control.

Consider this. It's fair to say some degree of accuracy can be found in each of the following statements:

- life isn't always fair
- bad things can happen to good people
- rain will fall in our lives
- failure can occur

It is equally legitimate and significantly more productive to appreciate:

- sometimes life is more than fair
- good things can happen to good people, and can be better appreciated as a result of the bad things
- the sun can, and will, dry the rain
- failure cannot occur without the decision to give up

Whether we choose to develop and maintain a constructive viewpoint or not sets the stage for pending perceptions and results. Some time back, I came across a newspaper article that effectively explored this, as well as the relationship between expectations, chance, and outcome. Essentially, the primary contention offered was that, from sports to scientific experiments to every-day life, expectations often dramatically influence results.

One case study spotlighted involved teachers informed that a group of students had scored well on an academic placement test. These teachers were further armed with the knowledge that, historically, test results had served as a reliable indicator of scholastic potential. Somewhat predictably, follow-up analysis months later produced telling results. The teachers consistently reported higher levels of academic development, motivation, effort, and achievement among the high-test-scoring group. By contrast, teachers recorded significantly diminished results for low test scorers. As evidenced by the documented accounts of lowered levels of comprehension, determination, and accomplishment, these students exhibited significantly less confidence and ambition than their high scoring counterparts.

While, at first glance, these results may not seem to be exactly extraordinary, the teachers were dumbfounded when informed that the original test results were falsified. In reality, the only classification criteria utilized for establishment of the test results groups was random selection. To what can we attribute the clear discrepancy in performance reported following the announcement of the test results? Did teacher and student expectations preempt what would otherwise have been the natural order of things? It would certainly seem so.

And were it not for the revelation of the falsified results, it's not difficult to imagine the long-term, life-altering effects such expectations could have had on the students—positive and negative. Further, it's entirely possible that modified expectations, and the resulting treatment, for even the short duration of the experiment still had a profound and lasting impact on the lives of at least some of the adolescents.

What if it's our expectations and subsequent responses to day-to-day circumstances that determine the tenor of our life's spiral? What if, when it's all said and done, we bear the lion share of the power, and even the responsibility for determining whether our personal spirals are heading up or down, challenging or limiting, rewarding or otherwise? What if?

A person's degree of happiness is the direct result of the sum total of a lifetime of individual perceptions and responses. As a result, what is paramount is how we choose to view and respond to our circumstances—and not so much the actual circumstances themselves. In other words, smile as often as possible, so perspective can more easily be found. Maintain unwavering belief in yourself in conjunction with an inspired effort, and life's ample opportunities and lessons will be more readily revealed. Spurred by these results, a new and empowering mindset will be attained, a mindset readily fueled by the newly nurtured positive messages from within.

Some might think this perspective is too simplistic—an understandable conclusion at which to arrive. Some would question whether fleeting concepts, such as individual happiness and personal fulfillment, even exist, not to mention being realistically attainable. These plateaus most certainly won't be attainable for those who choose not to believe. Ironically, as perceptions and expectations would also serve to affect their behavior, and eventually the outcome, they would in fact be living the theory, a spiral in reverse.

Simply put, quality of life comes down to attitude and countless self-fulfilling prophecies. And on the chance that we do possess any power whatsoever to influence our ultimate outcome, why would we ever choose any path but a positive one? Why would we ever elect to rob ourselves? We should choose instead to believe, challenge, expand, and explore, and we will most definitely experience a self-fulfilling spiral and prophecy fulfilled.

Happy spiraling to you.

> Each and every hour, endeavor to live every second of every minute for all it's worth, for time is precious. Whatever you choose to do with it, don't waste it staring at a clock.

Consolation from the Basket

Some time ago, I had a discussion with a young coworker regarding changes in her life. Excitedly, she informed me that she had finally committed, once and for all, to quit smoking for herself and her daughter. She enthusiastically declared that, while past attempts had been unsuccessful, the three days already behind her, and harsh realities of health concerns and plain-old maturity, would most certainly provide the necessary motivation this time.

I told her how proud I was of her, and offered assistance if she felt any hint of wavering or needed encouragement of any form. We discussed useful tools and preventive measures that could be utilized to maintain commitment, including the potential use of incremental rewards to keep her motivation flying high.

I saw her again almost a week later with her friend, and excitedly inquired about her status. Interrupting her light-hearted response, I added that I'd been looking out for her for a couple days, and clarified that my question had deeper implications than a recount of the day's events.

Somewhat dejectedly, she confessed that she had reverted back to her old routine several days before. When I asked, "What about all things we talked about, all the reasons you absolutely had to quit?"

She responded, "It was hard."

I began to ask questions intended to re-fortify her will and get her back on track again (including whether the reasons we initially discussed were no longer valid, why she didn't utilize the tools we discussed, was quitting still important, when was she starting over again).

With each successive question, what became ever more fascinating to witness were the effects of the "support" originating from the friend. With each pensive and unconvincing excuse uttered in response to the questions posed came another generous dosage of consoling justification from her friend. "She did try, but it was too hard for her, everyone was smoking around her, it's too hard to just quit," were among the complimentary excuses readily contributed by the friend. And while initially unsettled by my questioning, each new justification from the friend seemingly provided a little more ease to the young woman, each excuse seemed to foster a little more acceptance of things just the way they were.

I recall a perspective heard over the years about crabs in a basket. The story suggests that if crabs are left in a basket long enough, invariably, one will achieve some degree of success climbing out of the basket. Typically, the success is short–lived, however, as another crab virtually always pulls the climber back to the bottom of the basket.

Considered from that perspective, the consoling words of the young woman's friend, herself a contented smoker, suggests, while potentially subconscious, a more sinister motive for the otherwise seemingly uncomplicated and uninspired passing comments. Regardless of the intent, the effect of the friend's words was to provide cover from responsibility for failure while reinforcing the merits of the familiar and non-intimidating status quo. And with the inspiration to ascend to a greater self safely buried away, what is possible again becomes merely what already is. Aspirations are conquered and normalcy reemerges as life's settling force. Pressure to evolve is dissolved and fate remains the same for both the two young women, as well as all the crabs in the basket.

Something to consider before buying into any such consoling words offered on your behalf in the future.

No Concept of Defeat

Every award-winning song began with a note
Every Pulitzer-Prize novel with a blank sheet

Ever acclaimed artist started with a sub-par sketch
Every great dancer once moved with two left feet

In reality, every noteworthy accomplishment
Required essential elements in order to complete

Each example of excellence started with a dream
A dream and no respect for the concept of defeat

It Doesn't Just Happen

Do you typically read inspirational passages, or listen to motivational offerings just to find that, in the end, they don't seem to really help you? When exposed to inspirational offerings, do you tend to feel encouraged, maybe even a little inspired, but only temporarily just to have the feeling wear off after a short interval of time with no discernable progress to show for it? Has your resulting outlook caused you to seriously question the legitimacy and true value of uplifting messages as a whole? Are you coming ever closer to the conclusion that the lack of meaningful results is most appropriately attributable to the ineffectiveness of the passage or sentiment, if not to the general worthlessness of inspiring mumbo-jumbo overall? After all, you paused to diligently read the message and waited, and nothing came of it.

Exactly.

Consider this: simply reading or hearing a positive, inspirational, or insightful message and not actively endeavoring to absorb and make it a part of you is somewhat analogous to being a complacent "fan" for an otherwise favorite sport, never talking about your team, never cheering them, never jeering them when they're bad. The team's status doesn't materially matter one way or the other. There's no elation after wins, no dejection after losses. Each outing is watched without comment, energy, passion, or care. Not exactly an inspired fan—in fact, not exactly a fan at all. As the word "fan" is derived from fanatic, if that's the extent of involvement and commitment, what's the point? Why even waste time watching the team at all, or the sport as a whole for that matter?

Similarly, the argument can be made that claiming to desire improvement, yet not working to absorb and actively make use of each relevant, uplifting morsel of insight that comes our way is just as illogical and nonsensical. It takes more than passive reading or listening on our part. If we are not prepared to do the necessary work, to absorb and apply it, much like the scenario with the peculiar fan, what's the point of even investing the soon-to-be-wasted time?

In fact, if you have no interest in committing to the necessary work, in dedicating the required effort for improvement to take hold, you probably shouldn't even waste any more time reading this. If your mindset is such that you are not prepared to do the necessary work, there are probably more meaningful ways you could be spending your time. Life is too short to waste any more of it. Given that any recommendations to come would require effort on your part, it probably wouldn't be of interest. So if that description fits you, as you depart, let the remainder of us simply bid you a fond adieu.

You're still with us, great! It's good to see that you are prepared to do what it takes. It's good to see that you are committed to your happiness and fulfillment. Now, about that work... In reality, the actual work required is minimal. There are merely a few necessary steps required to absorb the uplifting message, to effectively incorporate it into your life.

First and foremost, we must be genuinely interested. Have you ever tried to retain something you weren't really interested in, something that didn't, in some way, have your thoughts aroused? Just consider the wealth of information presented over all our years of schooling. While it was imperative we concentrated on the information at the time, how much of that information was retained after the classes were over? For optimum effect, we must become passionate about uplifting messages and their potential to make a difference in our lives whenever, and from whomever, the insight comes. We should never cease to appreciate that each nugget of insight not only represents an opportunity for further growth and personal awareness but also the opportunity for us to move ever closer to our goals, to our dreams.

Second, we must wholeheartedly believe in, and be unconditionally committed to, the extent to which the collective impact of a lifetime of absorbed positive, motivational input can significantly enhance not only our outlook but our ultimate degree of achievement, even more, the very tenor of our lives. No obstacle or excuse can be permitted to derail the process. Nothing short of continuous can be deemed to be acceptable when the topic is one of personal growth.

Third, and most important, we should actively strive to make each meaningful, positive facet of the inspiring messages encountered a permanent part of us. How? Take the time to ask ourselves how can, and how should, the next inspirational passage, the next positive conversation, the next passing nugget of wisdom offered by a stranger on the street truly make a difference in our lives. We should ask ourselves what there is to learn from the insight and how it can be most effectively incorporated into our psyches. We should ask ourselves how our outcome can have the greatest impact, not only for today, but for years to come. We should ask ourselves how can, and how should, that impact be maximized to make a difference in the lives of others. We should then actively set about making the answers come to pass.

In the final analysis, if we make the most meaningful, inspirational insight a constant fixture in our lives, if we commit to the positive energy, embracing it with passion, commitment, and active deployment, we will most definitely be lifted. And with this consistent supply of energy to fuel us, our potential will be expanded. Our purpose will grow. Our lives will take on new meaning and a greater sense of fulfillment. Without a doubt, inspiration will come.

Just imagine the effect this could have in our lives, in the way we feel, in how we approach things, in what we aspire to, and in the degree of passion, to every initiative, we could bring. Just image what we could do.

Now, that's something to be fanatic about.

> With integrity, you are, and will always be, a winner in ways that a scoreboard can't even begin to reflect.

Dodgeball Anyone?

People are trying to ban dodgeball in schools. Yes, dodgeball, that simple little game we played as children long ago. While there are variations of the game, the overall objective remains—avoid being hit by the ball. Apparently, the people trying to eliminate its existence from various schoolyards and playgrounds across the country believe the game to be too harsh. In their estimation, the process of hitting and getting hit by the ball can promote feelings of aggression, increased competitiveness, dejection, and doubt.

Okay, what am I missing? It's a game. And to my recollection (it's been a little while since childhood), games typically have winners and losers. And depending on the game, some characteristic (intelligence, size, speed, ingenuity) is integrated with strategy, the will to compete, and sometimes a little luck to determine the outcome. It's a great feeling to be the winner—and it's not so great when we're not. If we should happen to find ourselves on the short end today, it is necessary we tweak our capabilities, strategies, and wills to compete more effectively and enhance future results. That not only sounds like a game of dodgeball, it sounds a lot like life.

Watching the news segment, it wasn't long before my perspective regarding the topic was complete. It seems, as a society, we spend so much time coddling our youth, eliminating challenging situations, avoiding exposure to difficulty, and formulating excuses for lack of performance, so that each successive age group is growing up less equipped to deal with the realities of life. This mindset is causing us to produce increasingly fewer adults with a healthy degree of respect for old-fashioned values like character, persistence, sportsmanship (win or lose), patience, humility, and a strong work ethic, not to mention good old mental, physical, and emotional toughness.

Some time back, I saw a health-related show analyzing the rising rate of physical illnesses, such as allergies, in teenagers and young adults. One theory proposed was that more and more children are being raised in sheltered ways, often now shielded from what, at one time, were the very familiar activities of playing in dirt, regular exposure to germs, and contact with whatever else kids get into. Lack of exposure at an early age to these harmful elements tends to result in the body's failure to develop the associated antibodies and immunities, resulting in less effectively equipped adults. Increasingly more adults are susceptible to what was traditionally inconsequential exposure. In other words, as J. Willard Marriott put it, "Good timber does not grow with ease; the stronger the wind, the stronger the trees."

Worse, we are becoming a society of entitlement. The tried and true concept of ideas, such as the value of personal effort, responsibility, pride in one's work, diligence, earning one's keep, and making one's own way in the world are increasingly giving way to today's feel-good perspectives of "recognize everyone," "everyone's a winner," and "reward the group, not the individual." What's the motivation for trying your best in such an environment? What is the motivation for personal growth, for getting stronger, for finding a new way? Think about it. One of the primary reasons for capitalism's success in the world economy is simply the fact that at its core is the construct that it's not everyone being equal that drives an economy; it's everyone having the opportunity to succeed, and being rewarded for their relative results. It's a simple yet powerful concept that has fostered unparalleled innovation and personal growth.

I'm not sure exactly where I was the day competition became a bad thing. Growing up in the inner city, the most stressful times in my childhood were competitive, whether in school, in the neighborhood, or at the playground. Because of those experiences, virtually nothing fazes me today in the corporate world because I've seen worse. Bullies and various other sorts, who didn't have my best interests at heart, had to be dealt with. Because of those times, I have more effectively been prepared for what may come along. And today, I wouldn't trade those lessons for anything.

My contention is that, as is evident with virtually every other species on the planet, competition facilitates individual growth, fortitude, humility, honor, and toughness. It is the foundation of the strength and ultimate accomplishments of the group as a whole. Lack of competition, on the other hand, is a formula for complacency, a what-about-me mentality, and a collective migration toward the lowest common denominator. Success, innovation, pride, aspirations, and belief in one's self are all important personal goals that inevitably lead to collective advancement for the society. And competition is the foundation that most facilitates enhancement, making optimum achievement possible.

In this changing world, increasingly stronger, more talented, more dedicated people will be required for us to continue to prosper. Our children will need to be stronger, more focused, and more passionate. Now is the time to change the trend, to introduce more competition in our children's lives, not less.

A little dodgeball anyone?

> True heroes forsake words in favor of deeds that say everything that needs to be said.

Living Life "Committedly," Regardless of *Webster's*

Okay, why is it, exactly, that "committedly" is not a word?

To appreciate the relevance of this we may need to fundamentally alter our paradigms about commitment. First, instead of viewing commitment as one or two significant steps, we will need to perceive it as a series of baby steps. To individually accomplish these baby steps, minimal effort is required. Yet as the results of the multitude of the achieved baby steps are combined, anything, including your most ambitious dreams and aspirations, becomes increasingly viable.

Over time, this new paradigm yields a new, more effective methodology for living a full and accomplished life—one that emphasizes an appropriate degree of concentration and spirited execution for each individual hurdle with the remainder of the race being allowed to take care of itself. We will come to appreciate that the best way to ensure a successful life is to appropriately approach each individual day. For if we confidently, energetically, and aptly approach and clear each individual hurdle, neither how we finish the race nor whether we make an impact will ever be in doubt. In other words, live life committedly.

- ### The Process

Incredibly, embracing commitment and instilling the necessary behaviors, tendencies, and expectations in your everyday life is anything but difficult. For starters, no momentous splash, and no unbelievable feat is required to begin. First, whether large or small, simply determine what steps are achievable this day. Then diligently set about checking them off, one accomplishment at a time. At day's end, take stock of each of your commendable achievements.

Begin the next day taking stock of yourself, your achievements, and your forward motion, vowing that day nothing less than more of the same. New objectives will be identified and subsequent opportunities yielded. Ever more inspired, you will dedicate time out of your day in a meaningful effort to address them.

And with stock taken that evening of your achievements, you will encounter your pillow and prepare for the cycle of commitment to, tomorrow, again lift and propel you. Take time to rest your motivated attitude and inspired perspective, however, for they will again, tomorrow, be crucial for fueling an ever-expanding cycle of commitment.

With each passing day, more tangible impact and consistency can be expected, each day compelling a re-invigorated will to grow. The more accomplished, the more your potential will be irreversibly elevated. New possibilities will seemingly propel you into each new challenging and increasingly fulfilling day.

In time, any perceived wariness of commitment will be completely eliminated as commitment's amazing potential is more implicitly understood. Instead, commitment will increasingly gain recognition as the energizing, motivating, and empowering force that it can be—capable of facilitating previously inconceivable direction, clarity, and purpose. That's the point when you will truly comprehend what it is to live life committedly. That's the point when true appreciation of your intended destiny can begin.

Amazingly, all it takes is minimal effort and a little consistency to start yourself down the commitment path, where your true destiny and ultimate fulfillment await. Yet none of it can, or will, be realized until you are committed enough to take the first step.

Life is short and time is fleeting. It's up to each and every one of us. A meaningful portion of the next twenty-four hours can be committed, dedicated to our dreams and aspirations, and focused on the tasks necessary for the fulfillment of our intended destinies. Or, a meaningful portion of the next twenty-four hours can be committed to worrying about what might go wrong, focusing on the past, finding fault, looking for excuses, or paralyzed in fear. Our lives can be defined by the exorbitant time we choose to dedicate to the familiar yet meaningless and unproductive day-to-day activities and pursuits, which will net us nothing except more wasted time and avoidance. Alternately, our lives can be defined by our tireless quest for the kind of genuine happiness and fulfillment that can only be realized with realization of our true purpose.

Either way, the clock is ticking, on both this unrecoverable day and your unfulfilled destiny. What you do from here is up to you. Are you prepared to do what it takes to begin living life committedly? Just know, whatever you decide to commit to, it's not only your choice, it's your life.

Think about it from this perspective— how much is truly at stake, and it becomes increasingly evident that it's not commitment that is worthy of our fear. No, what we should truly fear is the outcome and legacy of a lifetime of commitment to nothing. It doesn't get much scarier than that.

> Passion is the critical bridge over the perilous waters of doubt and complacency, which makes each and every meaningful goal achievable. Without that bridge, it's fair to say, for the most part, all hope is lost.

Maybe You Can Sing

We often witness people who have the ability to sing, dance, publicly speak, write, draw, perform, play a sport, and we think, "Wow, he or she is gifted." Every once in a while, we even quietly contemplate: "How incredible would it be if I could do that." Almost never, however, do we stop to consider we most definitely can do these things, only to different degrees. In the process, we fail to realize that the talents on display are not so much the result of supernatural genetics as they are the culmination of years and years of passion, dedication, sacrifice, practice, growth, and refinement. In other words, while a few of Michael Jordan's athletic attributes were gifts from above (height, for instance), without the countless hours of practice, sacrifice, and dedication through the considerably leaner years, his "Air-ness" would not have become one of the best players to ever pick up a basketball. To the world in general, chances are he would have been an unknown.

What we must begin to appreciate is that everyone who demonstrates notable proficiency at some talent or skill typically has managed to advance to that point via effort and development. While the capabilities on display may be impressive today, they certainly didn't start out that way. So the next time you find yourself wishing you could be good at something, stop and ask yourself, "What's stopping me?"

So go ahead and sing, if singing is your passion, demonstrating an unyielding passion come what may. While becoming exceptional may come in time, enjoyment, fulfillment, and improvement can be yours each and every day.

Mission 6

Today, take a little time to figure out a song or movie that most definitely qualifies as one of your all-time favorites. Spend some time reflecting on why, what is it about the song or movie? What place does the song or movie take you back to? Who or what does it remind you of? What memories, thoughts, and feelings come back to the surface? Since that time, where has life taken you? What do you miss? What are you happy you lost? What does all this cause you to appreciate? Contemplate these questions a little, then put them aside and experience it like never before. Enjoy.

Eventually, Death Visits Us All

Inevitably, death is a foe we all have to face. Ironically, coming to terms with it is vital to living a full and happy life. Though we can grieve it and those lost, it's also necessary we use it—to be more motivated, passionate, and happy, to be more appreciative of the time we have and the people we spend it with, and remind us to live every precious moment for every morsel of wonder, excitement, and love it has to offer. For we can run, but we can't hide because eventually death visits us all.

For Mom

Five years later and it still hurts. It doesn't take much either—a song, a movie, a random memory that happens my way—and I'm done. All of a sudden, I'm a grown man crying like a child, a child who has lost his mother. It wasn't supposed to be this way. And it still hurts. However, the reality is, my hope is that it will always hurt. Because I never want to lose the firsthand knowledge of how much I miss her or just how much she means to me.

And if you happen to still be blessed enough to be able to touch your mom's face, to hear your mother's voice, go to her, call her, do whatever it takes. Hug her, kiss her, tell her you love her this day and each and every day for the rest of your life.

And if it warms her heart, if she smiles, I'll take a little comfort in knowing my mom's passing has not been in vain.

Whatever you do, don't keep her waiting.

Whatever you do, don't wait too long.

In Time, All Answers Will Be Revealed

The Lord has summoned his child home
Away from all pain and worries
But why her, why now?
During this difficult time
Focus not on the questions
Carry forth her love and her faith
In time, all answers will be revealed

In the Upper Room

A close friend had an aunt whom, after months of proving a more-than-worthy adversary, appears to be succumbing to an increasingly debilitating bout with cancer. Unfortunately, many of the familiar signs were there—the inhumanity of late-night emergency-room visits, extended periods without the consumption of food, blurred lines of reality, and occasional exclamations of "being so tired." And for loved ones, the overwhelming feelings of helplessness, frustration, sorrow, anger, and fear continue to grow. In my friend's teary eyes I boar witness to the grueling yet unsatisfied search for answers.

This is the article I didn't think I would ever write.

Do you love anyone? I mean, do you really love anyone? I'm talking about the kind of love that has already stood the test of time. I'm talking about the kind of there's-nothing-more-important-in-your-life-than-your-love-for-that-person kind of love. I'm talking about the I-would-literally-give-my-life-for-that-person kind of love.

Well, that's the way I loved my mom. Above and beyond giving me life, she was the nicest, most giving, most humble, most down-to-earth, most loving person I have ever known. She had a smile that would warm any heart and a heart that made everyone she touched just a little better. I never knew of a time that she wasn't giving or planning to give again. There wasn't anything she wouldn't sacrifice for me and my siblings, for family, for friends, for her faith. She was the epitome of the most magnificent compliment that can be awarded to any being. She was a loving mother.

And there was nothing I wouldn't do for my mom if I could.

I walked into her room, took a single glance in her eyes and knew. One look told me everything I needed to know. Just a couple seconds and the unimaginable burden of life's most unacceptable truth would alter my destiny for a lifetime. My mom was passing on.

Nothing else mattered, not a month of prayers, not the power of positive thought, not the tears or spiritual encouragement of the best of friends, not the visitation of her children or theirs, not one passing medical expert or any of their ineffective diagnosis. Nothing else mattered. My mom was going to die.

Up to the second I looked in her eyes I was convinced she would beat her illness. There was no doubt that the plans we'd made for the shopping spree and the grand meal once she returned home was just a matter of time. The nurse had called me at work, saying I should hurry to the hospital, that my mother's system was shutting down."

I abruptly interrupted, "What do you mean? Do something. Where is her doctor?" But upon arriving at the hospital I saw her eyes and knew, nothing else mattered. My mom was going home.

I whispered, "Mom, it's okay. I understand. Thank you for everything. I love you."

Somehow, I managed to ignore every acceptable notion that I had ever had, every considerable feasible outcome of my mother's month-and-a-half hospital stay, which I had permitted to enter my guarded consciousness. Although she had stopped speaking the previous week, her eyes told me what had to be done. One look told me I had to let her go. It wasn't easy, but somehow I knew it was what had to be done. I have come to believe this was the most valuable gift I could have possibly given her. In the most selfless act I have ever even conceived, I told her it was okay to go. As a result, I know she knew that I understood. She was tired. She had accepted her fate, which her faith ensured was to a better place. She knew I understood that this was bigger than us, and beyond our control, that the harsh reality was that death is an inevitable result of every life.

I told my mother to go ahead home. I told her to say hello to her mother, her father, and so many other family members and friends who had preceded her. I thanked her for fighting so hard, and for so long, for everything she stood for, for making me the person I am. I then phoned my sisters, my brother, and my father. I informed each that she was passing, holding the phone to her ear as each uttered their tearful goodbyes. It wasn't easy, but it was what had to be done.

A halt was called to scheduled shots and procedures. After seven weeks of medical attention from an assortment of doctors, nurses, specialists, therapists, and such, my mom's condition was beyond their control. Mom's life was in the Lord's hands. And all I could really do was to align my faith accordingly. A short while later Mom was relocated to a private room. Once everyone else had vacated the room, I started her tape player. Sitting next to her, trying to fight back the tears, I tried to savor every contour in her face, the feel of her hand, her scent, her warmth. I felt the need to try to somehow create a memory imprint, a permanent recording to have for all time. I told her over and over how much I loved her.

Then it happened. As the room began to fill with Mahalia Jackson's spiritually moving rendition of "*In the Upper Room*," I realized Mom had just taken her last breath.

There would be no recovery. The horrible spirit of death had come and robbed the very life from my mother's body, and my life would never be the same.

I laid my head on my mother and, with tears now freely flowing, I sang "*In the Upper Room*" to her one final time. When the song ended, I rewound the tape to the beginning of the song and walked out to inform the nurse. Both nurses rushed into the room to check her vital signs. I followed, heading straight to the window. Looking up at the clouds through my tears, I continued singing "*In the Upper Room.*"

And it was then, in the most devastated and most humbled state of my life that *it* happened. I can't explain what *it* is. To this day, I still do not completely understand. All I know is that then and there, a feeling came over me. *It* was there, and *it* wasn't. I felt the amazing presence of something bigger, something more incredible than I could even begin to fully comprehend. Then, as quickly as *it* had come, *it* was gone, and so were any lingering doubts. With unmistakable clarity, I understood that Mom was in a better place; my mother was going to be just fine. There, for the first time in my life, I knew inner peace. It was there I came to appreciate that only faith would see me through.

Looking back on that day now, I'm amazed at some of my actions. I'm amazed that her eyes could tell me so much, amazed that I could maintain some semblance of sanity, of calmness throughout it all. What I am most proud of however, is the fact that I could overcome all my personal desires, fears, anger, frustration, and sorrow, and tell her it was okay. There was no guilt and no pressure, only acceptance, dignity, peace, and faith in the Lord. She went peacefully, knowing that I understood. She went, faithfully believing we would see each other again. It was the only fitting way to end such a beautiful life.

Because of its sensitivity, this is the passage I didn't think I would write. Because of my friend and so many others searching for answers, I knew I had to.

The Garden

It is said that Adam and Eve began in a garden
A state of paradise, perfect happiness they knew
But innocence expired as knowledge was gained
Regret would follow and the ache of sorrow too

And so too did I know a magnificent garden
With hope and happiness, no sense of true pain
No shortage of great aspirations for the future
In my life, dreams and confidence used to reign

But change did things, both big and small
Up went down, every purpose became another
Ignorance was stripped, my youth taken away
One fateful day, with the passing of my mother

Now I understand that everything can be lost
Loved ones simply taken, no rhyme or reason
Everyday is darker, things just aren't the same
Not living, not loving, not any event, or season

I offer this warning with the best of intentions
I encourage you, treasure loved ones everyday
Hug and love them as if there is no tomorrow
For in time, your garden of paradise too will decay

The Fringe

On the fringe is where I find myself
Somewhere in the mesh of life and death
Each breath the result of an ever-present fight
Truth is, life has descended to little else

Every day I hurt, this pain too joins others
Today another function my body can't perform
With family and friends visiting each day
The truth is most always I feel alone

On the fringe is where I find myself
It's hard to believe this has become of me
Friends mask smiles, but tear tracks are apparent
They inquire, but don't really want to know

Faith tells me loved ones wait with open arms
And for that I believe my heart rejoices
But my eyes see loved ones that don't comprehend
So I continue to fight—not for me, but for them

On the fringe is where I find myself
Coming to terms with my sins from the past
I've made my peace with the Almighty
I value each remaining moment, good and bad

And when the inevitable happens, someday before long
You should know that my time hasn't been in vain
Know that faith matters most in the think of the storm
Find love and be happy until this fringe is your own

Comfy

Every morning, before I face the world, I kneel next to where you lie. And with one hand on the Bible and the other on you, I pray. I pray for the world, for Mom, for me. In you I find comfort. With you I find the strength to face another day. Furry inanimate object or not, you have become my source of hope, my link to my meaning.

In my last year of college, I decided to test the corporate waters and attempt to earn some real money by applying for a coop. My first interview was when I first met Diana. Diana was a middle-aged, middle manager in a large corporation who never learned that to make it she needed to lose her humanity. In fact, I was pretty sure I was high on the candidate list when, in the interview, my summation of a previous summer job teaching children culminated with her in tears. I remember sitting there in awe of everything. I remember her saying, "If we hire you, we are going to have you do this, and this, and that." I remember thinking, *Okay, I don't have a clue how, but if you say so.*

I was hired, initially as a six-month co-op, then into my first post-graduation full-time position. Diana essentially took me under her wing, showing me the ropes, giving me magnificent opportunities and encouragement. Without a doubt, she had me doing this, this, that and more. For three years, she was considerably more than a manager. In many respects, she was closer to a second mom. I still recall the conversation we had when it was time for me to move on. With tears in her eyes, she congratulated me on my performance. With matching puffy eyes, I thanked her for the stage, to which she replied that she was sure, with or without her, I would have found my stage.

In my new role, I didn't see Diana nearly enough. After moving to another office, I heard through the grapevine she had been ill. Later, I was informed she had cancer. By the time I made plans to visit her in the hospital, given her advanced stage, close coworkers were warning me: perhaps I should not go. But I knew I had to see her no matter what.

I stopped in the gift shop on the way to her room, trying to get my thoughts together, trying to figure out exactly what I should say. The woman in the gift shop suggested a lightly packed stuffed animal. She told me people in Diana's condition like to have something they can squeeze, something they can hold on to. The salesperson also indicated that people visiting ill people instinctively want to hold the patient's hand, at times contrary to the patient's wishes. A stuffed animal sometimes eases that discomfort. I picked up a cute little puppy to be gift-wrapped. The puppy worked like magic. Not only did Diana like the gift, gratefully, she seemed to recognize me.

A few weeks later, when I visited a much weaker, less vibrant Diana, her daughter interrupted my clumsy introduction with, "You're the one who gave her the puppy! She really loves it. When she's awake, she holds it. When she's asleep, she holds it. When we take it out of her hand during her bath, she frets until we return it. Thank you." That day, I visited with Diana for the last time. She was holding the puppy.

Several years later, while visiting my mom during a short hospital stay for some exploratory testing, I again found myself in the gift shop. With warm memories of the way Diana had lit up upon receiving the stuffed animal, I decided on this life-like lovable furry Teddy Bear with a brown polka-dot ribbon for a tie. Mom loved him. She later told me how everybody thought he was so great, so unique. Mom also informed me that when it would get cool in her hospital room at night she would sleep with him on the exposed side of her face. She named him Comfy.

Comfy came home with Mom and found a resting place on her bed. Mom didn't have many local friends (since recently relocating to move in with me), but the ones she had saw and heard about Comfy.

Later that year, my mom's doctor informed me that she had suffered a stroke. We were advised that she should be admitted into the hospital for further testing. I remember not being overly concerned at the time because we could see daily improvements in her condition. She asked for Comfy the night we admitted her, but I apologized—I had forgotten him. I assured her that Comfy would be there the next morning and he was.

My mom took a turn for the worse after being admitted. Instead of getting progressively better, she became progressively worse. For the next month-and-a-half, I spent as much time as possible with her. No matter what, I stayed positive. I knew she would get better, the whole time Comfy was there watching over her and keeping her company. When she hurt, Comfy was there. When she slept, Comfy was there. When she went down to be operated on, Comfy was there. When she cried, Comfy was there. When she prayed, Comfy was there. When family and friends visited, Comfy was there. When we sang spiritual songs together, Comfy was there. When I sang spiritual songs to her because she didn't speak anymore, Comfy was there. When she died, Comfy was there.

Now, everyday before I face the world I kneel at Mom's bed and say a prayer. I ask God to take care of her and to give me the strength and wisdom to continue in her footsteps until I see her again. I thank God, tell my mom I love her and kiss you.

Thank you, Comfy!

She's Always with You

Her beauty is the vibrant remnants of the fading sun,
    in a darkening sky
Her touch is the gentle breeze, which whispers,
    "You're not alone"
Her voice is the rustling of trees, ever present,
    not to be ignored
Her scent is the enchanting aroma of a rose,
    fresh and unforgettable in bloom

Her pride is your inner will, a foundation for
    your convictions
Her spirit is the inspirations of offspring,
    present and still to come
Her faith is the source of spirituality,
    of your oneness with God
Her wishes and prayers are the reasons you will
    go on to strive for your destiny, your happiness,
    and true love

Whether through a magnificent vision,
    a grandchild's smile, a refreshing rain, or the next
    time an intermission in life causes you to become
    aware of the beating of your heart,
She's always with you
In every instance, whispering, she loves you

Any Day Now

For much of my life I've had an ever-present fear of death. Thinking back on it today, I believe more than anything it was really the fear of the unknown. It was immensely troubling to my young logical mind that the destination was uncertain. While grownups preached faith in a better place, I battled with thoughts, such as, *How do they know there's a better place, what if it's actually a permanent sleep or state of darkness, what if it is just the end*? Somehow I wanted to find a way to live forever.

At a very early age, I would struggle to stay awake at bedtime. I reasoned that as long as I was conscious I would, at the least, have a fighting chance. Years later, I remember listening to the church congregation gloriously singing, "Count the years as months, count the months as weeks, count the weeks as days, any day now, we'll be going home." I thought to myself, *Are they crazy? What is their hurry? Where is the cause for celebration?* They couldn't have known the outcome of death with any more certainty than I did. Didn't they realize that faith, by definition, is rooted in chance?

Growing up, movies dealing with the topic of passing loved ones regularly piqued both my interest and sorrow. As an adolescent, for instance, I can remember watching *Brian's Song* many times with my mom and crying every time. By adulthood, *Beaches* and *Boys on the Side*, and even a few songs, were producing similar mood-altering effects, sometimes resulting in me tearfully endeavoring to prepare for the impact of such a loss. This perspective caused me to more often consider the fact that any day could be my last. I believe I grew up more intensely focused on whether, on an ongoing basis, I was doing the right thing and the extent to which loved ones knew I cared. With each passing year, however, my questions only multiplied. Where does all of this lead? Why are we here? What is the purpose? Is there rhyme or reason? Does our existence really matter? How can some be seemingly blessed with so much and some with so little? Why do so many of the good have to die so young? Where is the fairness of it all? Is this, all there is? Why the sorrow? Couldn't this whole life-death thing have been implemented a better way? What is on the other side? Is there another side?

On a still very much unconscionable January day however, my fear and the lion share of questions about death ceased. With the last remnants of life dissipated from my mother's body, too went any surviving traces of innocence and doubt. No logic or intelligence could help me cope with the immense crater in both my heart and the pit of my stomach. Only faith saw me through the pain I could have never imagined, faith in her faith, faith in the Almighty, faith that if I followed in her path, I would see her again.

As a result, my daily concern became retracing the loving and caring life she lived, regardless of what the journey brings. My faith tells me that making the world a little better, as she did in her own way, is the only way to ensure I will see her again.

Shortly after Mom passed, I heard a minister tell a story about three young women sitting on a bench pleading with death to give them another chance. Death left, agreeing to give them a warning before he came again. Twenty years later, the three women, sitting on the same bench, were approached by death again. Each argued that it wasn't their time, that they had received no warning. Death reminded the first woman of a recent surgery that was touch-and-go for a while; and the second woman of a serious car accident a few years ago that she had walked away from. In both cases, Death indicated it was their warning to get their lives in order. The third woman asserted, “I’m different. I’ve had no accidents and no operations.”

Death responded, “Remember the first time you squinted to see something, your first gray hair, or the first time you couldn’t quite spring out of bed in the morning? You’re right, you are different. I’ve been giving you warnings every day.”

Perhaps, when it’s all said and done, the irony is that this life is simply about preparation for the next. In other words, simply put live right, be respectful, and be cognitive of your daily choices. The Almighty will take care of the rest.

Count the years as months.
Count the months as weeks.
Count the weeks as days.
Any day now, we’ll be going home.
See you soon, Mom.

Another Tear

If I should shed another tear,
Will it be any different today?
Will life have renewed meaning?
Will my mom be back to stay?

Will innocence be found again?
When I worried with whom to play?
Would life be simple like it was,
If my tears come again this day?

Would memories of bad deeds,
From my consciousness be astray?
Would hope and joy unseat them,
If yet another tear I refuse to delay?

I doubt things would alter much.
The truth is at times life is just gray.
Because of that and so many things,
I reserve the right to cry some anyway.

Mission 7

Listening to the radio one afternoon, I was perplexed by an ad. The commercial tagline was, "Play the lottery, give your dreams a chance." I thought, wow, obviously the state lottery officials believe the only odds the listening audience has of approaching their dreams are the unconscionable odds of winning a lottery. Worse, I thought how sad would it be if they were correct, if some people did perceive such limited chances and lack of influence over whether their dreams could come true. I guess we should thank our lucky stars that we don't fall into that classification.

Here's the mission: Today, identify one task, no matter how big or small, that can be accomplished today, one task that will take you one step closer to living your dream. Then set out to make it happen. In this way, we can again prove to ourselves that we are not among those dependent on the odds of a lottery for our happiness and fulfillment, for the achievement of our aspirations, for us to begin to approach our intended destiny. In this way, on this day, you will give your dreams yet another chance to come true.

And Faith Ensues

Faith is the intersection where everything comes together. There is faith in the Almighty. There is faith in self. There is faith that all this; life, death, and all the ups and downs between have purpose. There is faith that the appropriate perspective, decisions, and actions will bring true happiness and fulfillment in this life; that even greater rewards will come in the next. When it's all said and done, there is faith, and faith ensues.

The Event

Some time ago, a passing perspective expressed in a movie unexpectedly captured my attention, leaving an indelible heaviness lingering in its wake. The perspective was that there are a few significant events that single-handedly change the course of our respective lives. Our mindsets, our behaviors, our thought processes, nothing is the same afterward. From the point of the occurrence, every other event is gauged chronologically, as taking place before or after the life-altering one. I listened intently while nodding.

My event occurred one particular January evening, a number of years ago. My event happened when, with me in a state of utter helplessness, I realized my mother had just taken her last breath. To this day, tears can still flow from my eyes without warning as I think about the minutes before, being alone with the most beautiful and giving person I had ever known, silently praying for God to make her better. (My prayers were in spite of the fact that the doctors had diagnosed her "system" as shutting down, and had confessed there was nothing else they could effectively do.) Trying to come to terms with the fact that she was no longer with me, at least not in the form that greeted me when I came into this world, I realized I would no longer know the feel of her touch, the sound of her laughter, the sound of her song. I would no longer be able to hear my mom say she loves me. In a split second everything changed. In that split second, my mom was no longer here.

After that, nothing would or could again ever be the same. The better part of the next few years would be spent in various stages of anger, disillusionment, isolation, and despair. Well-meaning friends and family recommended I try to get out of the house, but being in the house (where she had come to live merely a few months before taking ill) was where I wanted and needed to be.

I may not have had many of the answers at that time, but one thing I was sure of was if I wanted to effectively come to terms with the sheer enormity of her loss, if there was any hope of finding any intended meaning, if I wanted to truly deal with the predicament and not push it aside and have it limit the remainder of my life, if I wanted to truly honor and appreciate her, I had to experience the pain completely. To my thinking, it was the only viable path to formulating answers to the pressing questions the event had managed to bequeath me. Why was she taken so soon? Why couldn't she have had a couple years of enjoyment after all the pain in her life? Why couldn't she have taken less care of everyone else and better care of herself? What else could I have done? Where was she? Was she in heaven? Is there a heaven and hell? What is the point of life? Why are we here? Why was I here? What is the rhyme and reason? Why should I even care?

Slowly but surely some of my answers became apparent. I say "my" answers because I'm not sure that, for everyone, the answers are the same. As I talked in depth with her friends, as I really began to take notice of, and truly appreciate, the things she held close, I realized that in spite of the pain, my mother knew happiness. Her friends helped me to see that she was full of laughter, love, and faith, and that she was proud of her single most important accomplishment, raising her children. I began to realize that, because of her faith, she was strong in ways that I am only beginning to completely comprehend and appreciate.

Along the way, I heard a story about a minister that seems appropriate to recount here. The minister upon hearing that three of his most ardent church members had died in an accident asked, "Lord, why? Why did you have to take three of my most worthy members? I would have gladly given up some of the others who clearly do not serve your name."

The Almighty responded, "They were never yours to give. I took the three because it was time and they were ready. I left the others so that you could get them ready."

My mom was ready. And I'm so grateful for the time I did have to share with her and the many lessons she taught me.

I have a considerably different perspective now. I no longer have the illusions I had about the possession of limitless personal power and intelligence. Reality, along with a dash of humility, has a way of setting in pretty quickly as you watch life seep away from someone you truly love. There is only one real controlling force. And any power or intelligence possessed comes through recognition and respect for that force. I believe the elders refer to this as faith. Ultimately, it was my mommy who taught me that.

I've come to realize something else since the most painful day of my life. I've come to realize that our purpose here is to learn, love, laugh, grow, and to try to make the world a little better every day we are blessed to be here. From my pain came thank-you letters for her friends and numerous discussions with others who struggled with life and loss, which led to inspired thoughts and inspirational passages, which led to the Web site, and so on.

Two objectives supersede all others for success. Via SomethingToShare.com, the books, and any other inspirational content to come, it is my hope to positively impact and influence the world, at least in a small way, while I'm here and maybe even a little after I'm gone. And second, wherever she is, and whatever she is doing, I want Mom to be able to look down on me and be eternally proud.

Ironically, the most amazing belief I have come to hold is that during the event, when I asked God to make Mom better, he actually answered my prayers.

In closing, I share something I contributed for the back of Mom's program:

None of us knows the volume of sand
remaining in the hourglasses of our lives

Now, more than ever she teaches us to
appreciate time. Now, more than ever she teaches
us to appreciate the people we spend it with

And with every gentle breeze that brushes my face I know that I am not alone.

The Path She Laid

As overwhelming as the pain may be
As untimely and unfair
Her summon to God's side
Find comfort

You were blessed to have her in your life

And as long as you treasure and mimic
Her laughter,
Her lessons,
Her love
Her impact will be everlasting

Follow in her path and have faith
You will see her again

> Faith is the bridge between our knowledge and God's wisdom.

Looking Up

Not so many years ago, I was on top of the world. I was a young man, a college graduate, in pretty good health, in a rewarding and well-paying career, with a positive attitude and the kind of confidence that just didn't waiver. My confidence didn't waiver when I decided to seek a more fulfilling job and received offers from each company I'd applied to. It didn't waiver when I accepted a job dependent on technology never supported before. It didn't waiver when, within a six-week period from receiving the job offer, I'd found and closed on my first house, relocated to a new state, and settled in to a new career in a completely different industry. Yep, things were coming together as planned. Confidence was in abundant supply. My perspective was, if I stayed positive, I had the power to do anything I set my mind to.

But wait, before you get the wrong impression, I most certainly wasn't self-absorbed, self-centered, or pompous. To the contrary, I considered myself very much fortunate. In an unassuming way, I endeavored to lead by example with a willingness to share my theories, concerning personal power, with anyone who was in need.

And no intended audience for that message was more important to me than my mom. On a regular basis, she found herself subjected to my self-empowerment beliefs, especially when she would use one phrase in particular. She would simply say, "I'm just going to leave it in the hands of the Lord." I can almost hear my rebuttal now: "Mom, the Lord gave you a brain, two arms, two legs, and everything else you need to solve your problems. You have to make it happen, not just sit back and wait for divine intervention." I would suggest to her that she needed to be stronger. I would advise her that she shouldn't just let things happen, that she needed to take control of her own destiny.

Two weeks into the new job, one week into the new house, I accomplished the most important goal of all. Mom relocated from another state and moved in. Finally, I could take care of the person who had dedicated so much of her life to me. Now, I could really lead by example, more directly challenge her to take control of her life and help her to be truly happy. I could work toward dissolving her financial worries, while supplanting any remnants with better opportunities for the future.

Shortly thereafter Mom took ill. Merely months later, she passed. So much for the plans of having better opportunities and hope for the future. So much for her having the opportunity to take control of her life. So much for all of my so-called personal power and for being able to accomplish anything I set my mind to. The bottom line was, when the chips were down and it mattered most, I couldn't do a darn thing to stop my mother from dying right before my eyes. I couldn't do a darn thing but cry and pray, pray that there was a heaven, pray that the Almighty would see her through, pray that I would see her again.

Isn't it funny that no matter how mighty and powerful we think we are, when the chips are really down, when danger looms, we eventually find our way back to the one and only true source of power: faith. My mom had faith. And it was only after her death, rivers of tears, at times seemingly endless pain and heartache, a little anger, a very much shaken foundation, and much contemplation that I came to realize that faith is what she was referring to when she would say, "I'm going to leave it in the hands of the Lord." She meant she was going to lean on her faith. Now I understand that she realized some things were simply beyond her control but never beyond the Lord's. Mom's philosophy didn't shatter in the face of a catastrophe, it only made her stronger.

I saw a movie entitled *Instinct* in which a prisoner unexpectedly grabbed a psychiatrist charged with evaluating his psychological health. Holding the point of the doctor's pen to his throat, the prisoner threatened to mortally stab the shocked and now very much frightened doctor if he could not tell him what he'd just robbed him of. The psychiatrist, fighting back the tears, responded that his control had been taken. The patient letting him off the hook and having made his point, corrected him, offering that it instead was his illusion of control that he'd lost. In effect, control is something we actually only think we have.

As for me, these days, I've managed to regain rock-solid belief in myself. Now, that belief is complementary to my belief in a higher power. Further, that belief has become more complementary to a rejuvenated sense of faith.

And the truth is the house, the job, the money, the prospects—I'd give them all up in a heartbeat to have my momma back to stay. If I had it to do all over again, I'd spend less time telling her what she needed to do and more time simply telling her I loved her no matter what. I'd spend less time worrying about what, or how, she would do in the future and more time finding out how she felt each day. I'd talk less and listen more. I'd attempt to teach less and endeavor to learn more. I'd think less and work on believing more. I'd tell her I was proud of her more than she could possibly say she was proud of me. I'd focus less on work and more on the time spent in her presence. And she would know more and more each day just how much she was loved. But the reality is that I don't have it to do over again.

I guess when it's all said and done, all we truly have are our memories, our passion, any wisdom we've managed to compile, our attitude, and the respective choices in front of us. All we truly have is our faith and ourselves.

Thanks for investing the time to accrue a little more perspective by way of the path I've traveled. And because you have, because of any renewed perspective, promise, faith, and enhanced happiness and fulfillment in your future, my new, most important mission continues to be fulfilled. We can be encouraged; for our futures now promise even more fascinating challenges and interactions in store. The power to influence our respective directions and outcomes is in our hands. Yes, things are most definitely looking up.

And as for anything beyond our sphere of influence, both from personal experience and per my mom, apparently, *His* hands are never full.

The Majesty

On occasion, let us set aside our computers, mobile
phones, pagers, all the technological advancements
of today's processed and manufactured superficial
world, to appreciate the natural inherent complexity
of the truly pertinent and meaningful world all
around us.
How do birds know to fly?
How do fish know to swim?
How do trees know to grow?
How do the seasons know to change?
Who decides patterns in each evening sky,
such magnificent masterpieces of purple, blue,
orange, and yellow?
How is each and every one of the billions of us so
intricately constructed, and so fundamentally
unique?
Majesty absolutely surrounds us every day.
And if we take time to respect and appreciate
the wonder of it all, through humility,
One day, we just might discover the glory of God.

The Rainbow's End

Unconditional love for everyone is the rainbow
Admission into God's kingdom is the pot of gold
Let faith and happiness guide you on the journey
And the rewards will be immediate and everlasting

Home

There I stood; looking out the door at the home I grew up in some three decades ago. And it was all a bit mind-numbing. There had been so many changes. Although so much of the present scene from that front door, witnessed countless times during my youth, was now foreign to me, there still was so much that remained intimately familiar. Immediately, my mood became reflective. What happened to time? Each new day seems to bring some new element of change. And while that's okay for each day that we migrate in the direction of that ever-present change, it seems something else, as in our yesterdays, are left ever farther behind.

I found myself thinking about my mother, whose loving touch and, too often, underappreciated ad-hoc words of wisdom I am no longer privileged to have. I could almost see her just up the street, in a lively discussion with one of the neighbors as happened so many times when I would come to the door to let her know someone wanted her on the phone, or to find out what she wanted from the store.

Standing there, I began to contemplate. If I had all the money in the world, some days I feel like I would gladly give it up to go back and simply relive a day, to relive that day, not worrying about what I didn't have or where, one day, I wanted to be. No, I'd relive that day simply fully appreciating what I had, appreciating the simplicity, appreciating the love. Things seemed so much simpler back then. In many ways, things seemed to make considerably more sense. Not only did the days tend to be longer, they seemed to be absolutely marinated in meaning. But alas, I had to catch myself and remember that the distortions of memory most often favor the days gone by.

Finding an unoccupied passenger seat, my reflective mood took the liberty of accompanying me on my drive back to my abode. For much of the trip, my thoughts were of the neighborhood, the many people, so many memories, so many sights and sounds that made my formative years so unique and special. Back then, the world was a different place, a much smaller, closer-knit, and more supportive and inspired place, and life moved at a different speed. That world appeared to know little of the lion share of ills, deficiencies, and sins of the world today. And those that *were* known weren't often discussed.

In that innocent world, I can remember wanting to find a way to live forever. In that innocent world, I couldn't understand anyone who didn't feel the same.

But, because life has a way of invariably moving on, time passes and change comes. Little by little, with the losses of youth, bliss, and ignorance, the cloak of innocence fades and what we are left with is the reality. In time, we come to learn favorite things can lose their novelty, wondrous places can fall victim to either neglect or an ever-fading memory, and even the people we love most can and will go away. We come to know reality firsthand. Soon enough, we come to understand reality isn't always kind. And one day, we look around and can't seem to find that innocent world we so well once knew.

Eventually, my attention drifted back into present day, and all around me, it was an amazingly beautiful day. Watching the majestic sun beam off the blue-green water, I found myself thinking that, as magnificent as the visions were before me, I probably couldn't, we probably can't, in this life, even begin to comprehend what true beauty really is, that there simply must be something beyond this life that is so much more magnificent than anything we could even begin to imagine. And I hope that's the ultimate reward.

It occurred to me that all of it must have a purpose. It occurred to me that this life, the ups, the downs, the things put before us, the things we achieve each and every day all must have a point. And while it's okay to reflect on the memories of the past, and it's okay to wonder what the future will bring, life is here and now, in the present. Life is appreciating what we've been blessed to have, being the best we can be to ourselves and those around us, striving to be happy in each and every moment and finding meaning wherever we can. Realizing this, I also realized that my quiet passenger had gone away.

To this day, however, I can't help believing, hoping, praying that my mom has found that place and that she's so happy. Now, I'm more than okay with the thought that, if I do the right things in this life, one day, in the next one, I'll be able to look through a very similar door, in a similar setting and see my mom conversing, for the first time, in all her majestic beauty. And I'll be sure to bask in that beauty for just a little while before calling out to her and igniting the celebration she has most definitely planned. Rejoicing at how good it is to see her again, I will come to know lasting fulfillment, for, after a life-long journey, I will have finally made it back... home.

> Every day is a blessing, and every blessing a gift from God. Spend your blessings wisely.

The SomethingToShare Daily Affirmation

I affirm that on this day I will...

Take the time to listen to the rustling leaves,
And to the passing breeze that made them so,
Marvel at just a bit of the majestic beauty
In the world around me,
And in some way rediscover the innocence of my youth.

I will tell, or better yet show,
A loved one how much they mean to me,
Help someone in need,
Immerse myself in that, which inspires me,
Strengthen my faith in the Almighty,
And strive to be someone in whom
The Almighty can have faith in return.

I will smile each and every chance I get;
And, whenever I can, bring someone else along for the ride.
I will endeavor to be modest as a rule,
But audacious when called for.

I will always know that I am here for a purpose,
And I will respect and appreciate this day
For the blessed and amazing gift it is.
I affirm that the precious time I have this day
Will be spent wisely,
I affirm, this day, zestfully will be the way I live.

continued at...

SomethingToShare.com

- and the world will be a better place

www.ingramcontent.com/pod-product-compliance
Lightning Source LLC
LaVergne TN
LVHW050624100826
845148LV00011B/1716